IMAGES *of our Past*

HISTORIC
CHARLOTTETOWN

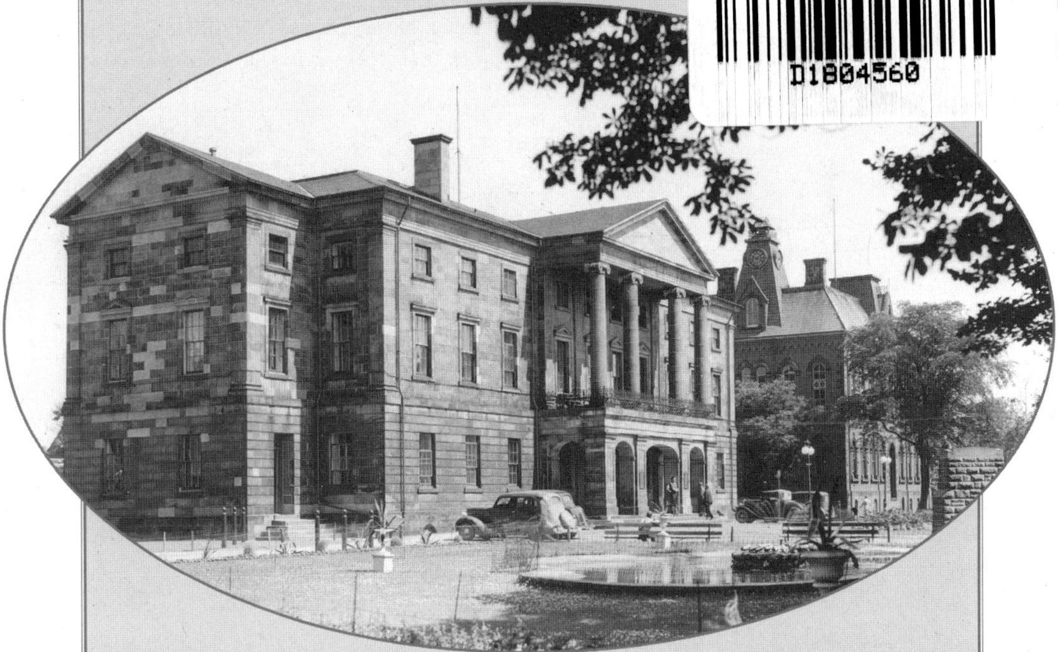

JULIE V. WATSON

NIMBUS
PUBLISHING

Dedication

*This book is for Tipsy
my companion exploring Charlottetown
your passing left a huge hole in my life and heart
how I miss the joy you gave me*

Copyright © Julie V. Watson 2007

All rights reserved. No part of this book may be reproduced, stored in a retrieval system or transmitted in any form or by any means without the prior written permission from the publisher, or, in the case of photocopying or other reprographic copying, permission from Access Copyright, 1 Yonge Street, Suite 1900, Toronto, Ontario M5E 1E5.

Nimbus Publishing Limited
PO Box 9166, Halifax, NS B3K 5M8
(902) 455-4286
www.nimbus.ca

Printed and bound in Canada
Design production: Margaret Issenman

Title page: Due mostly to the influence of Arthur Newbery, the assistant provincial secretary and amateur landscaper, Province House came into its own as a magnificent seat of government. The beautification of Queen's Square led to its position as the administrative centre of the Island and in 1872 Province House was joined in the square by the Dominion building.

Library and Archives Canada Cataloguing in Publication

Watson, Julie V., 1943-
Historic Charlottetown : images of our past / Julie Watson.
Includes bibliographical references.
ISBN 978-1-55109-599-8

1. Charlottetown (P.E.I.)—History—Pictorial works. I. Title.
FC2646.4.W38 2007   971.7'500222   C2007-902418-1

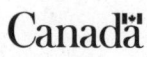  

We acknowledge the financial support of the Government of Canada through the Book Publishing Industry Development Program (BPIDP) and the Canada Council, and of the Province of Nova Scotia through the Department of Tourism, Culture and Heritage for our publishing activities.

Contents

Preface v

Acknowledgements. iv

Introduction—From the Forest a Capital is Born 1

Chapter 1—Birthplace of Canada 17

Chapter 2—Growth of a City 29

Chapter 3—Transportation 51

Chapter 4—Commerce and Agriculture. 79

Chapter 5—Culture and Community 97

Chapter 6—Sporting Affairs 119

Chapter 7—In Service to Others 131

Chapter 8—Answering the Call to Arms 149

Selected Bibliography. 167

Image Sources 168

Acknowledgements

A special thanks to the staff at the Public Archives and Records Office of Prince Edward Island who are not only helpful in finding those special items, but also make research an enjoyable experience.

Thanks to the many writers, photographers, artists, publishers, and others who have done so much to capture the essence of Charlottetown past. It is through their skills that I am able to create this look at historic Charlottetown.

Finally, thanks to Randy Flanagan, the Charlottetown Fire Department, Library and Archives Canada, and Karen Lavers and Mayor Clifford Lee of the City of Charlottetown.

Preface

One of the hardest decisions an author has to make is how to arrange a book—what to include and what to leave out. In this case, we are looking at the period from 1719 to the 1950s with more than two hundred years of history to choose from. In this book we can barely scratch the surface of Charlottetown and its citizens. Any single chapter or section could be expanded into a book of its own. There are so many details that could not be included, so many images that couldn't be shared. My wish is that you enjoy my selections, but that you also take advantage of the Public Archives of Prince Edward Island, our museums, libraries, and more importantly, our city streets, to further appreciate the past efforts that went into creating a wonderful city that we are proud to call home.

I am a person who enjoys linking the past with my present and who takes comfort and pride from early accomplishments. Thus I decided to build the book on what I feel are the photographs, stories, and past achievements that link yesterday with today.

Researching a book like this one brings out a great wish for a time machine. Charlottetown's past is one I could happily visit. It was never violent or marred by war, never torn by great conflict. There were a few unfortunate "incidents" and the painful effects of the great wars, but Charlottetown was generally a good place to live where people were able to concentrate on building a better life for themselves and for the next generation.

The next best thing to a time machine is to hit the streets and see how much of the past is preserved or can be imagined. Stand on a street corner and know that just over there stood a market or that across the street was the home of a Father of Confederation. Understand why houses near the waterfront sit close to the street and why such wide streets form rectangles within the old town. Think about how people lived an active outdoor social life to pass the cold days of winter.

When writing about the past I feel it wise to envision things through the eyes of the people of the era I am attempting to capture. To that end I began by envisioning myself on the deck of a sailing ship travelling along the southern coast of this island. After a few miles of shallow coastal seas the coastline indicates deeper water—an inlet or bay that can accommodate our vessel.

Passing between sandstone cliffs, narrows open to reveal a natural harbour. The Mi'kmaq called it Bootsak, meaning "narrow passage between cliffs." The French built a fort here, Port La Joie, on the west side of the narrows; the English later renamed it Fort Amherst. This magnificent harbour widened to a basin with three rivers flowing into it. To build a settlement on the land situated between what we now know as the Hillsborough and North rivers, looking out towards the narrows and the West River, would have been an easy decision in the 1700s. This settlement would, of course, become Charlottetown.

Almost three decades ago when my love for the history of Prince Edward Island was in its infancy, I was rummaging through some old books and came across one called *John of The Lilacs*. It was old and worn, as if often thumbed through. I paid my few dollars, took it home, and realized I had a treasure. John of the Lilacs, a.k.a. John Robert Campbell, published a collection of his poetry in 1940 and did much to capture the essence of a past era, what so many love about Prince Edward Island and its people and, with these words, what so many treasure about our capital city.

Charlottetown

Here Nature etched indeed a place of beauty
With restful vistas, viewed on every hand;
With panoramic scenes of sky and water
Of red, red cliffs, of trees and fertile land:
Nursed gently on the breast of gulf's blue waters,
Upon this Crescent Isle—this land of home,
Here is the wanderer's rest! The Artist's glory
This jewel radiant within the ocean's foam.
Historic buildings aging, grace our city.
Church steeples and cathedral's stately spires;
With sundrenched streets, a wealth of leafy shade—
Green foliage that flames with autumn fires.
Here parklands greet the whispering tides of ocean
With scent of leafy mould—of flower and fern;
The summer's fragrance—the autumn's fiery grandeur—
All blend where thoughts' great pyre of memories burn.
Within time's loom in Charlottetown were woven
The robes of nationhood that gown our land!
The golden bonds of unity from North to South—
From East to West which nation's form have spanned!
This lullaby with ocean's ebb and flowing,
Sings of our Island dear where beauties blend!
For here within this peaceful cherished haven
Is Charlottetown—Her Capital—Your friend.

Introduction

Early Beginnings: From the Forest a Capital is Born

Charlottetown's past is inseparable from the early history of Prince Edward Island as a whole. The two are forever entwined due to the role Charlottetown played as the capital of the colony and later of the province. It is common belief that the first Europeans to arrive at Prince Edward Island were John Cabot and his crew in 1497, although some believe the Vikings preceded them. Although a second explorer, Jacques Cartier, also came ashore in 1534, European settlement to the island was slow to begin. In fact, it was not until almost two hundred years later, in 1719, that the French permanently settled Port La Joie across the harbour from present-day Charlottetown and named the island Isle St. Jean.

First Residents, N.D. Sally Mitchell, Mi'kmaq, is shown at Rocky Point across the harbour from Charlottetown. Not a lot is known about her, but these photos depict a strong woman of dignity wearing traditional dress. The headpiece's appearance in photos taken many decades apart suggests it was used for special occasions.

BASKET MAKING AT ROCKY POINT, N.D.

Trade quickly developed between the first residents and the citizens of Charlottetown. Mi'kmaq baskets and outdoor furniture were particularly valued.

The Mi'kmaq people resided on Prince Edward Island for thousands of years before Europeans arrived by living off the land and sea, something that became more difficult after settlers came to the island. By 1875 the Mi'kmaq population had dwindled to about three hundred. Some of the remaining Mi'kmaq lived at Rocky Point, across the harbour from Charlottetown and near the original Port La Joie. Formerly hunters and gatherers, the Mi'kmaq saw their way of life changed forever, and many produced baskets and other handcrafted items which they sold in the capital.

ROYAL WELCOME, c.1860

When His Royal Highness, the Prince of Wales, arrived in Charlottetown, the Mi'kmaq community was part of the welcoming ceremonies, and rightly so. The native peoples who had been so helpful to Europeans when they arrived were an accepted part of the community, having long inhabited the area around what is now Charlottetown and the Hillsborough River. In 1917, several acres in the same vicinity were made into a reserve. In 1972, this and two other reserves (Morell and Scotchfort, located further up the Hillsborough) were renamed the Abegweit Band, one of two First Nations bands in Prince Edward Island.

 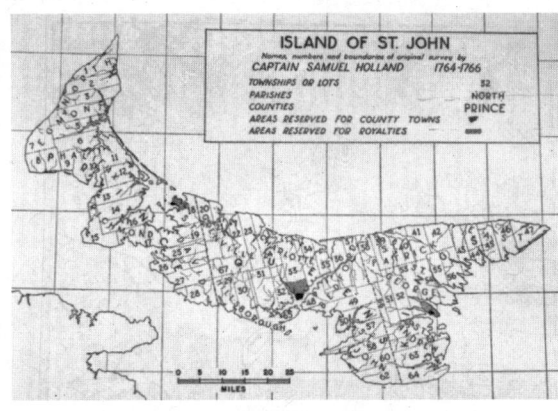

LEFT:
CAPTAIN SAMUEL J. HOLLAND

In 1745 the small colony was captured by the British. Three years later it was back in the hands of the French, but the Treaty of Paris ceded "permanent ownership" back to Great Britain in 1763, when it was placed under control of the government of Nova Scotia and renamed St. John's Island. Recognizing the fisheries potential of the colony, the British had the island surveyed by Captain Samuel Jan Holland in 1764.

Born in Holland in 1728, Captain Holland followed his ambition and quest for adventure to England. When Lord Louden was appointed commander-in-chief of the British forces in North America, Holland accompanied him to the colonies, an act that undoubtedly led to Holland subsequently being appointed surveyor general of North America. Holland was instructed to proceed with surveying Isle St. Jean first, so he moved to Observation Point (also known as Observation Cove and now called Holland Cove) and from that base divided the island into lots. His plans were sent to Britain in 1765.

RIGHT:
HOLLAND'S VISION OF THE ISLAND OF ST. JOHN

Holland's survey divided the island into sixty-seven townships, or lots, of about twenty thousand acres each, fourteen parishes, and three counties. The British government decided to grant townships to those who had claims for military or public services but so many applied that lots were drawn in London on July 23, 1767, with one hundred proprietors granted almost the whole island. "Charlotte Town" is shown on this map (black portion on the south shore, just below lot 33) as the site proposed for a capital.

OBSERVATION POINT, N.D.

Holland's home in Observation Point, across the harbour and just west of Charlottetown, is the scene of one of Prince Edward Island's enduring ghost tales. When Holland's lover, Racine, a woman of Mi'kmaq and French origin, set out to find him after he was late returning from a winter expedition, she disappeared. Mourning her loss, Holland searched in vain for his beloved. One still night the following summer, the captain's coxswain was wakened by low voices in the sitting room. Curious, he lit a tallow dip, and peered into the room. To his surprise he saw Racine seated on the knees of a figure in the captain's chair. At his approach Racine rose and fled, leaving behind an "odour of sea damp, a pool of water by the chair, and a trail of moisture" described as "the track of her dress." He also heard the words, "Why doesn't he come?" Holland and others again searched for her, but to no avail. For years, those courageous enough visited Observation Cove looking for Racine, and some even reported seeing the apparition.

CHARLOTTETOWN'S NAMESAKE, QUEEN CHARLOTTE, c.1765

Charlottetown was named after Queen Charlotte, wife of George III. Charlotte Sophia was born in 1744, married in 1761, and died in 1818, leaving nine sons and six daughters. This portrait by Dusan Kadlec was commissioned and presented on behalf of the Government of Canada at the commemoration of Charlottetown City Hall as a national historic site, July 1, 1988. Today, Queen Charlotte's coronation crown is still part of Charlottetown's coat of arms.

Charlottetown, despite a modest population of only about 250, was officially designated the colony's capital in 1765, based at least partly on Holland's reasoning that "as this side of the Island cannot have a fishery it may probably be thought expedient to indulge it with some particular privileges." The area's southern exposure, and the fact that the land was suitable, dry, and gently sloped to the water—unlike the harsher shoreline of much of the rest of the Island—were in the site's favour. So, too, was the availability of fresh water from nearby springs. The site, across the harbour from Fort Amherst, was sheltered, and the harbour was fed by three rivers, with the narrow harbour mouth easy to defend. The West, York, and East rivers quickly took on important roles for transportation, as sources of food, and as places of commerce. The East River, in particular, was a vital part of life. The Mi'kmaq called it Elsetkook meaning "running close by high rocks." The colonial British later renamed it the Hillsborough River for the Earl of Hillsborough. Two large groups of English settlers arrived and established themselves on the Hillsborough: Glenalladale settlers (Catholic Scottish Highlanders) landed on the north side of the river in 1772, and the Monaghan Irish arrived on the south side fifty-eight years later.

During British colonial rule, it was the English settlers who controlled the capital. Many Islanders today are descendants of British colonists who came to the Island either as proprietors or as agents to administer the colony and develop its land. During the first century of Charlottetown's existence, the British had the best access to education, the most capital, and the best training in agriculture, business, and fishing. As a result, most of the greatest merchants, shipbuilders, professionals, and for a time, the overwhelming majority of legislators, were English.

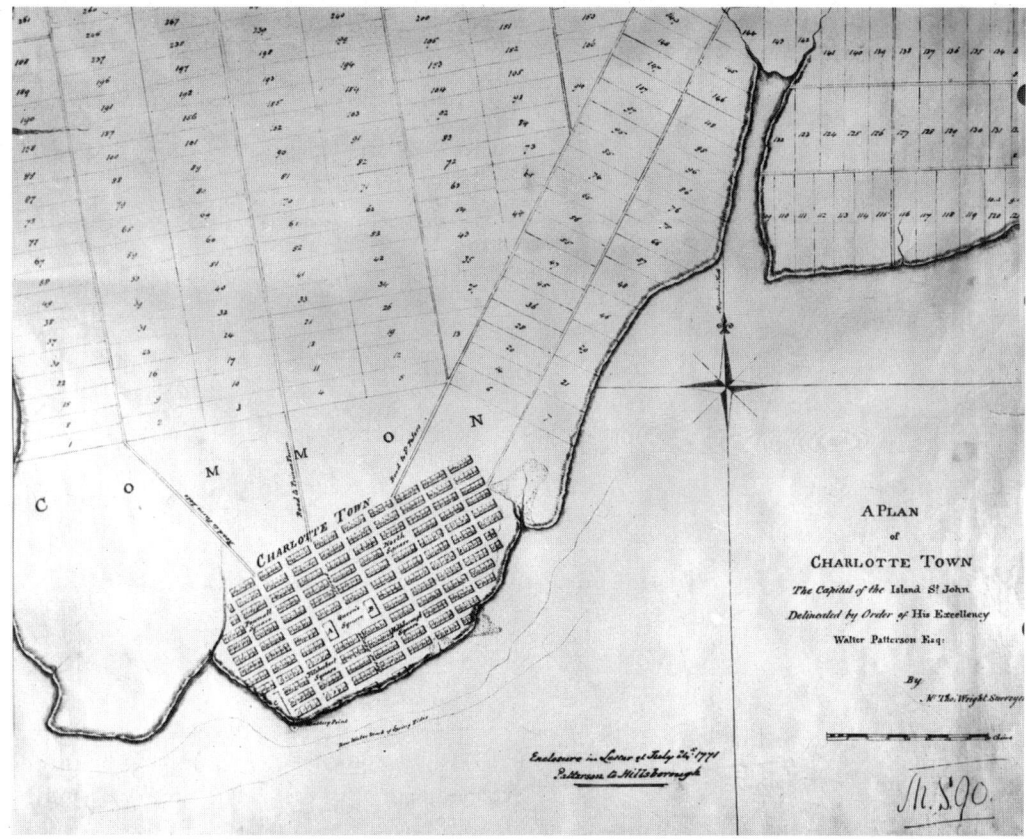

Lot Plan of Charlottetown, c.1771

Captain Charles Morris was sent from Halifax in 1768 charged with the task of planning the town. Morris put quill to parchment creating a town plan, which he laid out using what were, at the time, new theories of design. Wide streets for fire protection were set in a grid, with a large central area set aside for public buildings, parks, and squares. A year later, on June 28, 1769, the colony, already with a capital, was given a government of its own that was separate from Nova Scotia's.

Surveyor Thomas Wright later expanded on Morris's plans, creating five hundred lots and four public squares in his design. The plan pictured here is essentially that drawn by surveyor Thomas Wright. This original plan clearly shows how precise the guidelines were: the size of town lots (84 by 120 feet), roads (principal streets fronting the river are 180 feet in width and all others 80 feet) and the placement of important buildings were all outlined in Wright's design. Today, the city still largely reflects these original plans. The wide streets in the original plan were to provide protection from fire, recognized as the gravest danger faced by residents. The wide streets are still prominent in the city today.

Prince Street, showing Wright's wide streets, c.1930

When the town was laid out, it comprised 270 acres of building lots and 565 acres for a common, which allowed for future expansion. Because, as one early official put it, "every man must be something of a farmer to supply his family with milk, butter, roots and all other vegetables, until there be a market, which we cannot expect will be the case soon," the lots were spread out and provided with ample pasture. Streets were named primarily for British royalty and colonial officials, but housing was slow to appear as land had to be tilled first.

Surrounding the city of Charlottetown, and located within the historic boundaries of the eighteenth-century city plan, were the five municipalities now known as Sherwood, Parkdale, East Royalty, Hillsborough Park, and West Royalty, and just across the Hillsborough River, the community of Stratford. The Island population may have been small in the eighteenth century, but it was soon finding its voice. Some seventy landholders successfully lobbied the British government to be allowed to govern themselves, and in June of 1769 the colony of St. John's Island was declared independent of Nova Scotia.

One of the first public buildings in Charlottetown was the Crossed Keys Tavern, at the corner of Queen and Dorchester streets. The first Legislative Assembly of the colony was held there in 1773, making it the second-oldest English legislature in what would become Canada more than a century later. That first assembly of some eighteen members met for ten days and passed a few acts that dealt with important issues of the day: banning the sale of rum and other liquors without a license, planning for public roads, and establishing a supreme court. The tavern's proprietor, Alexander Richardson, was appointed the legislature's clerk, for he was a schoolmaster and a learned man. The tavern was also home to early sessions of the Masonic Lodge, Protestant services, and was probably the location of the Island's first school (held in a coffee house that was part of the tavern).

WALTER PATTERSON, THE FIRST GOVERNOR

Irish captain Walter Patterson, appointed governor-in-chief of St. John's Island, was given proprietorship of lot 19 with his brother and arrived at Fort Amherst in 1770. Two months before leaving England, Walter had married Hester Warren of Stratford and appears to have named his farm at Rocky Point after her, calling it Warren Farm. When Patterson arrived, the Island was in a very primitive state, but he worked hard under every type of difficulty during his sixteen years in office. When Patterson arrived from England he had to build a house to keep out the cold and like all officials, he had to bring his food, utensils, and furniture with him. With wooden vessels unable to handle the ice and crossings on foot made impossible by areas of partly open water, Governor Patterson determined to set up winter mail service. In the winter of 1775, the service became successful with the use of a canoe, which could cross both patches of open water and hard ice relatively easily.

Patterson travelled to England in 1775, hoping to spend about a year abroad straightening out the colony's finances. He would spend five years off the island, with Phillips Callbeck acting as governor in his absence. In 1781, after many island proprietors consistently failed to pay their annual "quit rents," a special tax for land owners, Patterson passed a law in the assembly permitting the acquisition of any land "at quit rents overdue," making bitter enemies of the proprietors. His personal and political enemies agitated for his recall and he left the Island an embittered man.

BOOK OF LAW, c.1701

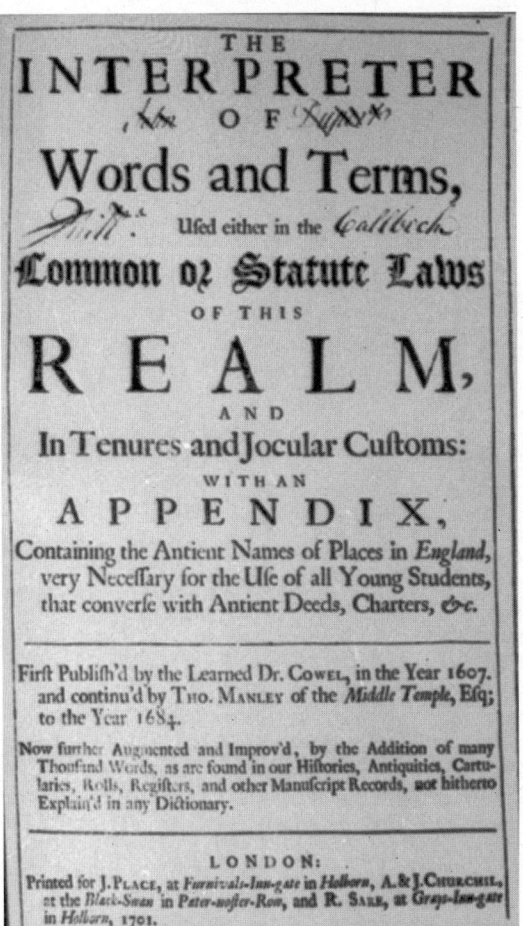

The most valued possession of men responsible for handing out justice would have been their book defining the law. This is the title page of a law book first published by Dr. John Cowel of Cambridge University in 1607. The edition shown here was printed in 1701, and was brought to the Island by the first chief justice, John Duport, who died in 1774. Its next owner was lawyer Phillips Callbeck, who came to the Island in 1770 as its first Attorney General. He later became president of His Majesty's Council and was acting governor from 1775 to 1780. In 1775, the only act of war committed against the colony's capital occurred when American privateers attacked Charlottetown on November 17. In addition to looting the town, they kidnapped Callbeck and his clerk, stealing all their personal property and taking them to George Washington's headquarters in Cambridge, Massachusetts. Callbeck was soon released, but all his possessions, including the very important provincial silver seal, were taken from him, making it a struggle to return home. The law book was the only piece of Callbeck's personal property that escaped the pirates' raid. He did make his way back to the colony, where he developed a winter ice boat that ran from Wood Islands to Pictou, Nova Scotia, raised and trained a militia, erected batteries, and laboured hard to break the system of land tenure. In 1790, the man known as the "Great Benefactor" died at age forty-six.

LEFT:
REPLICA OF THE LOST PROVINCIAL SEAL

RIGHT:
PRINCE EDWARD, C.1798

In 1798 an act was passed that changed the name of the Island of St. John to Prince Edward Island. Prince Edward, Duke of Kent and father of Queen Victoria, was commander-in-chief of His Majesty's troops in British North America. Edward had never visited St. John's Island, but he had ordered the building of new forts to defend Charlottetown Harbour and the construction of a new barracks to house two new companies of soldiers.

Development in the city, though, was slow. Any monies sent to the colony from Britain were used to pay the salaries of officials, leaving little to improve the town. One of the keys to city development was the waterfront. Since the beginning it was thought that the harbour would never be a significant port—it was not deep like those in Halifax and Saint John, nor was there room for manoeuvring a large fleet of sailing vessels. It did, however, become adequate for the burgeoning town, and welcomed many new immigrants to the Island throughout the eighteenth and nineteenth centuries.

The waterfront was especially important for an island colony. Almost as soon as Europeans decided to settle PEI, they were trying to figure out how to get off the Island in the winter. Even in the 1700s, being cut off from delivery of mail and supplies for the duration of the winter was hard to bear. Simple travel from settlement to settlement relied on open water, at least until roadways were cut and bridges were built. As technology improved, new methods became more common, but in Charlottetown's early days, winter travel often consisted of slogging across the ice.

It must have been an exciting time for Charlottetown's citizens when ships carrying newcomers tied up at the wharf. Unfortunately, not everything being carried by the ships was welcome in the city. In early 1847, *Lady Constable* out of Liverpool was loaded with some 419 souls fleeing the Irish famine. Typhus had killed twenty-five during the voyage and eight more soon after arriving. Even though the ship was placed in quarantine, another fifty-three passengers were later infected.

GOVERNOR CHARLES SMITH, C.1815

Charles Douglas Smith is generally regarded as one of the worst lieutenant-governors PEI ever had. Beginning in 1813, he ruled for eleven years with almost no assembly, instead putting his immediate family in positions of trust. Smith is perhaps best known for producing "Holy Dollars," or "Ring Dollars." As there were no banks or bills of exchange on the Island, merchants had to send cash for goods purchased in Halifax and elsewhere. The consequence was that silver dollars left the Island faster than they arrived, causing a great scarcity of coins. It occurred to Smith that if the centre were punched from each coin, then worth six shillings of local currency, the number of coins represented would be doubled. After punching, the ring would pass for five shillings, and the centre piece for one shilling. Being rendered unfit for circulation anywhere else, the coins would stay for use in the community. An order of council would have been all that was necessary to effect the measure, but there was some doubt that Smith bothered with this step. Coins were duly punched, and before long a canny Charlottetown man by the name of Mr. Birnie discovered that Lieutenant-Governor Smith had made his punch too large and that the silver in the centre pieces was worth more than one shilling. He carefully collected as many as he could, placed his treasure aboard a ship to be sent to England and sold, and eagerly awaited the return of his booty. Birnie was to be disappointed. The ship went down in the mid-Atlantic, taking his profit with it.

LIEUTENANT-GOVERNOR JOHN READY

Of course, not all governors were bad: Lieutenant-Governor John Ready was a complete contrast to Smith. During his time in office he did all he could to promote the welfare of the colony, and when his term ended petitions were sent to England by all parties to have him retained. He encouraged agriculture by importing animals for breeding purposes, he recommended inland post (which subsequently ran once a week during the summer), and he urged attention to roads, which were subsequently extended and improved. Still, few Island roads were fit to carry wagons, and trips to Charlottetown from rural areas on the Island could take several days. One rural resident remarked: "If I go to Charlottetown I am led into dissipation there and return home with an aching head, an empty pocket, and a half-starved horse."

As more roads gradually connected Charlottetown to the rest of the Island, wagons and carriages brought increased commerce, communication, and social exchange between town and country. Charlottetown became more urban in character as pasture lots gave way to buildings, increasing dependency on the supply of rural produce. While early residents of Charlottetown were government officials and military personnel, they were soon followed by immigrants from Ireland and Scotland, and Loyalists from America. Tradespeople like carpenters, blacksmiths, and artisans marked the beginning of industry, and a thriving agriculture was quickly established. A wharf was built in Charlottetown to facilitate trade by sea, especially between Princetown, Georgetown, and other Island ports, as well as the mainland. More ships came directly from overseas, bringing new colonists and supplies and returning with mails and timber. As the ships became bigger, larger wharves were built, along with cargo sheds.

Agricultural production grew, as did a trade in timber valued for export and the construction of homes, buildings, and ships. In the early 1800s, sailing ships were built in Island ports, filled with timber, fish, or agricultural products, and sold, often overseas. Shipbuilding brought prosperity to Charlottetown that continued until the middle of the century and the arrival of steam.

By the 1800s the Island was almost self-sufficient. Leather from local cattle gave employment to shoemakers, harness makers, saddle makers, and furniture makers. Wool from a large sheep population was made into cloth and used by tailors, dressmakers, and merchants. Charlottetown never became what could be called a manufacturing town. Instead, its economy was built on services, trade, and small production facilities, many of them tied to the fisheries, agriculture, and tourism.

English, French, and Mi'kmaq peoples made up a large proportion of early Charlottetown's population—people of Irish descent made up forty percent

OLD BOG SCHOOL, c.1880

A bustling black community existed in Charlottetown from 1810 to about 1910 in an area known then as "The Bog." Much of this land now holds provincial government offices and residential areas. When slavery was abolished in the colony in the mid–1780s, the black population chose to live near Government Pond—a marshy area outside the city—because they could not afford to live in Charlottetown. By the 1880s most people living in the Bog were native Islanders. In winter, Government Pond provided a great skating surface and residents quickly formed a hockey team, the West End Rangers, which regularly played other black teams in the Maritimes. In 1900 the team even played the Abegweits, Charlottetown's popular amateur men's team.

The Old Bog School, located in the west end at the corner of Kent and Rochford Streets, was erected in 1868 and closed in 1900. Sarah Harvie was the teacher at the time this photo was taken.

---

of the population by 1864. Blacks and Germans arrived in the 1700s, then Lebanese in the 1800s, and a small number of Chinese immigrants by the 1890s, and Jewish settlers arrived in the early 1900s. Most, if not all, of these people came to Charlottetown seeking to improve their lot, leaving less agreeable conditions for the freedom to pursue a good future for themselves and their families. Still, population growth in Charlottetown was slow until the 1820s. In 1768 the city had only 50 residents, mostly military personnel. That number grew to 416 in 1798, 2,063 in 1827, and 3,000 in 1830. By 1855 the population had doubled to 6,500.

As the colony grew, local people increasingly began to take part in public affairs. As the authority of the governor declined, citizens began to push for a democratic system. For eighty years, the British had handed some

George Godfrey, World Champ, c.1885

One of the most famous Bog residents, George Godfrey, was born in 1852 and became famous as a boxer. He left PEI in his youth to work as a porter in Boston. It was there that he started boxing at Professor Bailey's Hub City gym. At age twenty-six, Godfrey began fighting competitively in the bare knuckles tour. He made his professional boxing debut at Harry Hill's notorious music hall, winning his first fight. At 5' 10" and 175 pounds, George "Old Chocolate" Godfrey went on to become the World Coloured Heavyweight Champion, fighting in more than one hundred bouts.

---

authority to govern and collect taxes to local government in the form of a legislature and cabinet-style of government. Still, British officials retained ownership over most land and thus ultimate power. The lots that had been created in 1767 had been almost exclusively presented as gifts to those in royal favour, rather than to people with an interest in the development of a far-off colony. Many lot owners' total involvement with the island was collecting rent from its citizens. As a result, absentee landlords were certainly not conducive to improving and developing property. Citizens wanted land reform and the rights of freehold tenure so strongly that occasional rioting required the militia to intervene. The issue caused turmoil for many years, and in fact, the land question was not settled until after Confederation when the Dominion government loaned the Island enough money to buy out British land owners.

By the mid-1800s Charlottetown had become a busy town of wooden houses and stores, wide streets, and numerous squares and parks. A cityscape was forming, steered by Thomas Wright's original plans. City blocks in the area closest to the water began to fill in with houses, although it was the end of the century before housing density reached the level seen in the old town today. In the area close to the waterfront, houses and businesses were built close to the street while those away from the water had spacious grounds and were set back from the street, often with gardens in front. Houses were heated with coal or wood fires, and tallow candles gave light until they were replaced by gas.

Chapter 1

Birthplace of Canada

A CITY IN THE MAKING, C.1865

This photo of Richmond Street, near Province House, shows how the town had developed by the mid-1800s. A number of churches, a jail, and Government House were all established. Schools, including Central Academy that became Prince of Wales College, St. Dunstan's College, a grammar school, and infant schools began to take in students. The Colonial Building (later renamed Province House) opened its doors to members of the legislature in 1847. In 1852 the Charlottetown Gas Light Co. was incorporated by a group of local businessmen. Within a year, sixty homes had gas light.

In 1855 the legislature passed the City of Charlottetown Incorporation Act, which made Charlottetown a city and gave it municipal administration. The mayor and ten "common councilmen" were empowered to make bylaws for the "good rule, peace, welfare, and government." Police protection, fire control, lighting, and the regulation of markets and amusement houses were all placed in their care. During early elections, passions would intensify, and occasionally brawls would break out between Grit and Tory. Some think it was the consequence of election brawls, particularly one known as the Belfast Riot in 1847, which led to the Sons Of Temperance being organized in Charlottetown. This and similar groups eventually brought prohibition to the Island.

It took a number of years before the council truly became effective as it was hard to attract the right persons to run for office. The council was also forced to operate within limitations imposed by the colonial government, particularly the limits placed on the city's ability to gather revenue and spend money. As the city grew and as the municipal government gained experience, the council took on its rightful role of working for constant improvements. Discussions began immediately in 1855 about the need for a new building to house the fire and police departments and the civic administration offices. Construction began that very year. City legend tells us that, at one time, the third floor was used as a dance hall. Many of Charlottetown's other early improvements were driven by crisis. The great fire of 1866, probably the most serious crisis in the city's history, led to the enlargement of the fire department. A small pox epidemic in 1885 resulted in the installation of a water and sewage system.

POPE TAKES TIME TO EXTEND WELCOME, C.1864

In the 1850s the possibility of a union of the provinces of British North America was proposed, but at first Islanders were not in favour and refused to discuss it officially with other provinces. A decade later PEI did agree to discuss the formation of a Maritime union and to host a meeting in Charlottetown on September 1, 1864. Ontario and Quebec (known at the time as the province of Canada) asked if it might send delegates to see if that proposed union could include all provinces. The request was honoured and seven "Canadians," led by John A. MacDonald, made their way to Charlottetown to be unofficial observers.

The visiting politicians were officially met and welcomed by William Henry Pope, who was rowed out to meet them with all the dignity and decorum that he could muster under the circumstances: "in full command of an imbibing oyster boat with a barrel of flour on the bow and two jars of molasses in the stern, he presented greetings breathlessly and the Canadian delegation came ashore and landed." This depiction, *Prelude to Confederation*, painted by Rex Woods, shows the "Fathers of Confederation" on the deck of SS *Queen Victoria*, the ship that carried them from Quebec City to Charlottetown in 1864. The conference earned the city the honorary title, "Cradle of Confederation" or, as Islanders like to brag, "The Birthplace of Canada."

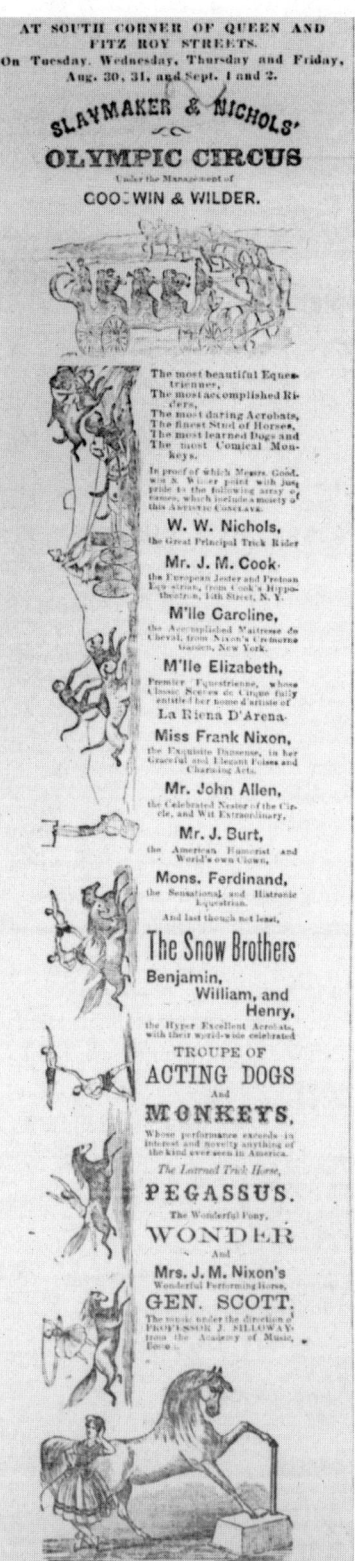

CIRCUS ADVERTISEMENT, C.1864

Few people in Prince Edward Island placed much importance on the gathering of politicians or their discussions. No special preparations were made, and there were no advance arrangements for accommodations or entertainment. When a large steamer, the *Queen Victoria*, anchored in the channel of Charlottetown Harbour, word of something unusual spread through the town. But although there was more coming and going at the Colonial Building and Government House than usual, the event didn't immediately garner much attention. The city's ten small hotels were filled with Islanders who had flocked into town for the Slaymaker and Nichol's Olympic Circus, which had set up tents nearby. It wasn't until the circus packed up its acrobats, and performing horses, dogs, and monkeys, that townspeople turned to the social events associated with the visiting statesmen. Luncheons, banquets, receptions, and balls held at Government House, the Colonial Building, and the homes of the host delegates set the tone for the conference.

POPE FAMILY OPEN HOME, c.1864

Hon. George Brown, delegate from Canada (now Ontario) was accommodated at Ardgown, the home of William Henry Pope and his wife Helen. Historians are forever indebted to Brown, who captured the spirit of the meetings in Charlottetown in letters to his wife, Anne. In one letter Brown wrote: "Cartier and I made eloquent speeches—of course—and whether as a result of our eloquence or of the goodness of our champagne, the ice became completely broken, the tongues of the delegates wagged merrily, and the banns of matrimony between all of the provinces of the B.N.A. having been formally proclaimed and all manner of persons duly warned then and there to speak or forever after hold their tongues—no man appeared to forbid the banns and the union was thereupon formally completed and proclaimed!" Ardgowan is now a national historic site, with gardens open to the public.

There were glowing reports of sumptuous banquet tables laden with "oysters, lobster, champagne and other Island luxuries," and the ball was called "The most brilliant Fete that has ever occurred in Charlottetown." For a time it seemed the caterer, John Murphy of the North American Hotel, received as much press as the politicians. He certainly earned a place in history as one of many responsible for creating a memorable atmosphere as Charlottetown entertained its visitors.

CONFEDERATION CHAMBER, C.1948

Confederation Chamber, where the 1864 meetings took place, became a Canadian historical site, attracting visitors from all over the world. Little is known about the proceedings in the Council Chamber of the Colonial Building, now known as Province House, but we do know of the final result. It was decided that Maritime union was impractical but that a larger scheme was feasible. The group decided to meet again in Quebec in October 1864 for further discussions. The most important achievement of the Charlottetown Conference was the building of goodwill between the delegates. It was a chance to get to know one another, to actually meet the other statesmen and discuss common goals and concerns. In an era of slow travel, such meetings were rare.

THE "FATHERS" OF CONFEDERATION, c.1864

This photograph, taken by G. P. Roberts of Saint John, was published with the caption: "Convention at Charlottetown, Prince Edward Island, of delegates from the legislatures of Canada, New Brunswick, Nova Scotia, and Prince Edward Island, to take into consideration the union of the British North American Colonies, September 1, 1864."

In the chief stateroom of the *Queen Victoria*, amid the wineglasses and cigar smoke, twenty-three men had taken the first steps toward founding a new nation. "Other states might have a more dramatic start—but few, surely, a more enjoyable one," wrote J. M. Careless. Negotiations that continued after the Charlottetown meetings, first in Quebec, then in London, England, led to the British North America Act. The act established the Dominion of Canada on July 1, 1867, bringing together what are now Nova Scotia, New Brunswick, Ontario, and Quebec. Prince Edward Island, ironically, declined to participate.

WILLIAM HENRY POPE, C.1873

William Henry Pope was a lawyer and colonial secretary under a Conservative government that enacted a policy of "nondepartmentalism," designed to combat patronage. In his political career, Pope took on difficult issues: property and land rights, reconciling religions, and confederation. Pope was one of few Islanders in favour of colonial union, an unpopular position that created havoc with his political career. He attended both the Charlottetown and Quebec conferences of 1864, but eventually resigned his position in the legislature in 1867 after his brother, Premier James Colledge Pope, passed a resolution against Confederation. But William's advocacy of railway construction on the Island indirectly led to the province joining Canada. Pope was also well-known for being editor of *The Islander*, a conservative newspaper, for thirteen years, and as a very successful judge. Pope was preparing a history of PEI at the time of his death in 1879.

JAMES COLLEDGE POPE, C.1873

William Pope's brother, James Colledge Pope, a prominent businessman and politician, and PEI's premier in the late 1860s and early 1870s, did not share his brother's enthusiasm for Confederation. James did not attend the Charlottetown or Quebec conferences, and as premier, he favoured the concept of Confederation but felt the initial terms were not as favourable for PEI. Pope let it be known that an increase in proposed funds for the purchase of absentee land holdings, a continuing problem on the Island, could sway PEI toward union. Pope's Conservatives lost the 1867 election but three years later formed a coalition government when the Liberal government collapsed. Pope's coalition began railway construction, an initiative his brother William had long supported, however the costs soon spun out of control, and ultimately forced the Island to seek terms for union with Canada. Despite an election defeat in 1872, by 1873 Pope's Conservatives regained power with a promise to obtain even better terms for joining the new nation. Somewhat ironically given his initial lukewarm response to Confederation, James Colledge Pope was premier when PEI joined Canada on July 1, 1873.

When Premier James Pope passed a resolution to build a railroad without the aid of the Canadian government, there was a great celebration in Charlottetown. The *Islander* reported a great torchlight procession through the streets of Charlottetown led by firefighters. A volunteer band played and a huge bonfire blazed merrily in honour of the occasion: "This procession, if not the largest, was certainly the prettiest thing of the kind ever seen in this City, and was universally admired for the unexpected and brilliant effect produced by it, and the excellent order maintained by the young men of which it was chiefly composed. Guns were occasionally discharged and sky-rockets were sent whizzing through the air...Several buildings on both sides of Queen Street and in other parts of the City, were also tastefully illuminated..." The first sod for the new railway was turned in October of that year. But all was not smooth sailing: route selection was a contentious issue and the cost was substantial.

Ultimately, the tremendous debt incurred from attempting to build a railroad was enough to push PEI into Confederation. The basic terms, negotiated in part by James Pope, were:

1) the Island would have six seats in the House of Commons
2) Canada would assume the province's newly created debt
3) $800,000 would buy out absentee landlords
4) there would be continuous communication with the mainland (in the form of steam ferries)
5) the Dominion of Canada would take over and operate the Prince Edward Island Railway

FAIRHOLM IN THE WOODS, CORNER OF FITZROY AND PRINCE, C.1860

As a newly created province, PEI gave Charlottetown new powers of taxation that helped the governing of the city become more effective. With more money to work with, the city quickly began to make improvements that were long overdue. Charlottetown's streets were one of the most visible signs of improvement. Layers of stones were laid down and compacted in what was called macadamization. For the first time, citizens could step off wooden sidewalks onto a solid surface, instead of the mud that had been common for almost 150 years.

The city's first cement walk was installed at Fairholm in 1894. Hon. Thomas Heath Haviland, sent out from England as an officer in 1823, a member of His Majesty's Executive Council, and later, Colonial Secretary, built Fairholm in 1842. Benjamin Rogers purchased the house in 1893, and one year later replaced the plank walk (shown in the photo on Prince Street) with the cement walk. Fairholm is now a national historic site and houses a five-star "National Historic Inn."

BIRD'S EYE VIEW, 1878

This sketch of Charlottetown gives an overview of life as seen by artist Albert Ruger and how he envisioned it in the future. Note the train entering the city via a causeway. The pond was later filled in to build the second station yard. As well, paddle wheeler the *Heather Bell* and other ships of the era are seen in the harbour, as are the many wharves on the waterfront. Ruger travelled to create what were known as bird's eye views, or panoramic views, of many communities. The artist walked the streets taking note of details to incorporate into his work.

Charlottetown celebrated its new status as provincial capital by laying the cornerstone for a new city hall in 1887. The inaugural meeting of the council in the new chamber was held on December 10, 1888. Now a national historic site, City Hall was built in the Romanesque revival style of architecture, and is still in use today. This grand building replaced the first town hall, a small wooden building located at the west end of Queen Square. Originally serving as the courthouse and then as a flour and meal market, it was built circa 1810.

Chapter 2

Growth of a City: Queen Square to Government House

GOSSIP AND A FILL-UP, C.1880

Town pumps were important for more than water supply. In fact, they were sort of like coffee shops today—a place to meet and greet, exchange gossip, and catch up on the local news. The pumps were important not only for consumption by man and beast but also for fighting fires. If fire broke out, bucket brigades formed from the pump to the fire. Water was also supplied to the city by water carters, who would bring barrels of water from Spring Park to sell for a cent per bucket. Their business thrived whenever it was thought there might be danger of the wells being contaminated—probably at the time of spring runoff or summer heat. The pump pictured is in Rochford Square; pumps were also found in Queen Square and on other principal streets.

As a new city rising out of the wilderness, Charlottetown was given the best of two worlds. Precise planning before inhabitants arrived fostered the incorporation of Old World amenities and the avoidance of mistakes learned from those who went before. Perfectly rectangular blocks with wide streets and plentiful public space would arise in orderly ranks from the harbour. At the heart of the settlement would be a square for public buildings: legislature, market, courthouse, and established church. Charlottetown's centre would be Queen Square.

OLD MARKET SQUARE, C.1845

This sketch of Old Market Square, from the talented hands of one Mary Caroline Bayfield (Mrs. Edward Bayfield), from the northwest corner of Grafton and Queen streets, shows the round Market Building with Province House in the background. For many years it was thought that the small building to the right was for storage, but further research at the Charlottetown Fire Department has determined that this and similar sheds around the city were where the all-important firefighting equipment was kept.

Though the plan was laid down in 1770, Queen Square remained a field for a couple of decades. The infant colony was all but bankrupt and money earmarked for public buildings had to be spent on other things such as the governor's salary. The first building finally appeared in 1795 when the Church of England's congregation erected a church on the west end of the square. In 1813 it was joined by more public buildings—a small market hall and a courthouse. Although the former had originally been planned for the waterfront, convenience encouraged a Queen Square site. In 1835 the Anglicans commissioned a new church. Tearing the old one down, they built the new one at the east end of the square and called it St. Paul's. In 1823 Charlottetown replicated its first Market Hall with the noted Round Market, which remained in use until 1867.

Mary Caroline Bayfield, c.1850

Mary Caroline Bayfield was of an artistic nature and gave watercolour painting lessons to a group of Charlottetown ladies. Historians are indebted to her for recording what the capital looked like in the early days.

"O Yes! O Yes! O Yes!" c.1860

With the ringing of his bell, the town crier would impart announcements to the general population. Shown in front of the old courthouse in Queen Square, this crier has a sheaf of announcements in hand. The insignia of the bell on his sleeve meant he had to abide by strict regulations governing how he conducted his trade. Walking about the town, he would pause to cry, "O Yes! O Yes! O Yes! Hear Ye!" followed by announcements or news, and finally the words, "God Save the Queen," for this was the era of Queen Victoria.

A minor civic official, the crier played a vital role, and because of the service provided and the prominent uniform bearing a bell crest, was a very prominent personage in the town. Communicating news or sharing details of a coming event was not a simple task. Criers walked the dirt streets of Charlottetown, pausing to ring their bell and call everything from government regulations, court verdicts, ship landings, arrival of goods, coming events—literally any news. In the beginning there were two types of criers. One crier carried the news of the courts and was known as the court crier. The other, the town crier, carried the news of the mayor and corporation (city), as well as that of businesses and private citizens. John Hatch, the last of the town criers, saw his job made unnecessary by newspapers, but continued crying well into old age. After losing his sight he was aided in his task by his grandson.

COLONIAL BUILDING, C.1865

In 1837, when lieutenant-governor Sir John Henry expressed concern about the PEI legislature meeting in private homes and taverns, there was warm support for his suggestion of a new building that would provide safe custody of public records. As one door keeper of the legislature remarked, the present system made for a "damn queer Parliament." It was voted that five thousand pounds be set aside to provide a building. Isaac Smith, a leading Island architect and builder, won the competition for the task. Stone was brought from Nova Scotia for the impressive three-storey seat of government, which was completely built by Island craftsmen. To make room for the new building, the Round Market was moved twenty-two feet to the northwest.

The cornerstone was laid in 1843 and the Colonial Building, which we now know as Province House, became the focal point for politics, public gatherings, special events such as visits by royalty, and even public demonstrations. The legislative assembly still meets here, although portions of it have been set aside to preserve and present the past and commemorate the role it played in the formation of Canada.

Second Market House, c.1902

In 1867, after a great deal of bitter debate, Charlottetown replaced its decrepit Round Market. Known as Butcher's Market, after designer Mark Butcher, its ground floor was divided into three sections—one for butchers, one for country produce, fruit, and fowl, and a third for meal and flour. The upper storey was finished as a public hall. The building also accommodated City Hall from 1872–1888. The Legislature, unwilling to share the square any longer with the "noisome market," insisted it be separated from Province House by a new street, Market Lane. The Confederation Centre of the Arts now occupies this land.

Parading Past Queen Square, c.1870

This area of Queen Square, taken from Queen Street towards Richmond Street, now houses the provincial library. During the 1860s and 1870s, owing to its success as Charlottetown's commercial centre, the appearance of the square created a bit of a furor. It was called "disgraceful, looking more like a farmer's pig pen or cow yard than the ornament to the city which the Public Square should be." By the 1870s, the south side of Queen Square, which we know as Victoria Row, was one of Charlottetown's main commercial streets. Businesses lining the street in that decade dealt with a variety of goods and services including tailoring, the selling of dry goods, and the manufacture and sale of rubber boots and furniture. Sale of rubber boots was probably brisk each spring when roads became a quagmire. Unfortunately, a fire in February, 1884, destroyed all but the building located on the corner of Richmond and Queen.

DIGGING OUT AFTER A STORM, C.1880

Streets were dug out by hand after a major snowstorm, with the snow left to melt and turn the streets into a quagmire. This photo, of Grafton Street on the north side of Queen Square, shows what a task it would have been. The clay that is predominant in Prince Edward Island made for muddy streets in the spring and fall and dusty streets in the summer. The poor condition of Charlottetown's streets was the main source of complaint from the citizens.

GREAT GEORGE STREET, C.1884

This view of Great George Street, from Province House to the waterfront, shows the city's tree-planting efforts. The little white fences are protecting seedlings which grace the city streets to this day as magnificent trees. The Fathers of Confederation would have walked up this street from the waterfront, but it isn't known if the wooden sidewalks were in place then.

The new sophistication reflected in the local citizens and the grand new buildings being erected was not reflected by the well-worn, poorly tended square. While the Colonial Building was majestic for its day, set among a nice orderly town grid, its grounds were nothing but ragged patches of grass, cut through with dirt paths that had little sense of order. Manure from the Market Hall was offensive and caused legislators to tread carefully. The square had no gardens, no trees, and "nothing to redeem it." The town's desire for beautification was undoubtedly stirred by a lecture given by the flamboyant Oscar Wilde in the Market Hall in October, 1882. The belief that planting trees would create barriers to prevent fires from spreading also helped with the city's beautification effort; unkempt squares would be no more. Another catalyst for change was a new practice being followed in Nebraska, where an Arbour Day was designated in 1872. A group of Charlottetown's leading citizens established the Charlottetown Arbour Society in May of 1884, an occasion inaugurated by planting the five public squares with selected trees.

ARTHUR NEWBERY, c.1890

Arthur Newbery, the assistant provincial secretary, and one of the province's few civil servants, became the driving force behind the Queen Square committee, devoting much of his life to its beautification. Raised in a home where art and beauty were highly prized (it is said that his father gave Robert Harris his first painting lesson), Newbery became an amateur landscaper. Between his devotion and skill and the city's support of Arbour Day, a transformation occurred. An article in the *Boston Globe* in 1887 glowed with praise: "One of the finest bits of landscape gardening can be seen in Queen Square. It is the work of a young artist, Mr. Arthur Newbery, whose office looked upon the barren waste until with his own exertion he reclaimed the desert and gave to the City a more beautiful garden than any publicly supported in all the Dominion." His work earned him the Imperial Service Order in 1905. His gardens became a popular attraction for both tourists and town citizens.

Province House, c.1930

With Newbery's influence, Province House came into its own as a magnificent seat of government. Queen Square finally assumed its position as the administrative centre of the Island and in 1872 Province House was joined in the square by the Dominion building. Designed originally as a courthouse, the Dominion building became home to the Dominion government offices after Prince Edward Island entered Confederation in 1873. This meant the courts had to find a new home. This was provided in 1876 when the law court building, now known as the Hon. George Coles Building, was built to the east of Province House.

DESBRISAY'S APOTHECARIES HALL, C.1924

The Apothecaries Hall was opened by Thomas Desbrisay, Jr. in 1810 on the northeast corner of Queen and Grafton streets and marks the northern boundary of Queen Square. It was likely the first non-doctor-owned drug store in North America. For many years it was the only place Islanders could get medicines, prescriptions, over-the-counter drugs, and even the ingredients to mix their own medications for both humans and animals. The cannon in the foreground of this photo (standing upright behind man in lower left corner) had fallen off the bank of Rocky Point when the block house at Fort Amherst was dismantled. It was salvaged by and placed it at the front of the drug store. During the Prince of Wales's visit in 1860, the Union Jack could be seen flying from its mouth. The cannon remains in place to this day.

THIRD AND FINAL MARKET BUILDING, C.1910

Charlottetown moved into an era of superb architecture from 1880 to 1930 with W. C. Harris, whose touch was especially prominent in Queen Square. In 1884 fire destroyed the Dominion building, and its replacement, the Cabot building, was designed by Harris. In 1895 a new St. Paul's, also designed by Harris, was built. In 1902 fire claimed the second Market Hall. The city held a competition to select a new design, and Harris won. The Cabot building, the Harris-designed Market building, and the Robert Harris Memorial Library and Art Gallery (built in 1930) were all eventually replaced by the Confederation Centre of the Arts.

Royal Welcome, c.1869

Royal visits were never treated lightly in Charlottetown. Great elaborate arches, such as these which welcomed Prince Arthur, were typically built along the official party's route. Along with several arches, bunting, flags, and wreaths of evergreens would decorate the route, which usually led to Queen Square where official greetings would be extended and great crowds would cheer the royals' welcome. Royal visitors and other dignitaries were usually housed at Charlottetown's other great building, Government House.

GOVERNMENT HOUSE ENTRANCE, N.D.

In its early days, the entrance to Government House truly gave the impression of a remote country estate.

In 1789 a parcel of land was set aside by Governor Edmond Fanning with the stipulation that it be used as the site of the residence of the lieutenant-governor. The hundred acres, known as Fanning Bank (later Fanningbank), included farmland to be used for the resident's food production. Government House, the official residence, was completed in 1834 in the Georgian style. The white, wooden-shingled building, one of Canada's most impressive official residences, has a spectacular view of Charlottetown Harbour. Fanningbank's front steps have been captured on film many times when dignitaries came to stay in the Island's capital. The front steps are perhaps most famously captured in the photo taken of the delegates to the Charlottetown Conference of 1864, the Fathers of Confederation.

EARLY PHOTO CAPTURES THE "ROYALS," C.1860

In 1860 when Albert Edward, Prince of Wales and future King Edward VII, visited Prince Edward Island during a tour of North America, a levee and afternoon party were held in his honour at Government House. This photograph is one of five images found in an old trunk in the Duvar home. They had suffered considerable damage from dampness and mold, but are still highly valued as images of early Charlottetown. Extensive restoration work was done by Mr. Porter prior to their donation to the provincial archives.

STEPPING IN FOR VETERANS, C.1915

During World War I, Government House and its grounds were offered to the federal government for use as a convalescent home for veterans. A new building, built on the east side of Government House and connected to it by a passageway, was named the Rena MacLean Memorial Hospital in honour of one of the Island's war heroes. The hospital contained four large wards of fifty beds each, while Government House provided the space for administrative offices, an operating room, and a few private rooms. After the hospital was closed about 1920, it was made available to the Charlottetown Hospital following the fire of November 22, 1921. In the basement of the memorial hospital was a vocational training school.

RENA "BIRD" MACLEAN, C.1914

Nursing sister Rena Maude "Bird" MacLean, daughter of Senator John MacLean of Souris, was born June 14, 1879, and lived a life of adventure and humanitarian effort that earned her acknowledgement as one of many Island heroines. She became a registered nurse and a nursing sister and was a head nurse when she enlisted with the Canadian Army Medical Corps at the outbreak of World War I. During the war, she was assigned to various hospitals in England, France, and Greece. In March of 1918 she was assigned to the *Llandovery Castle* hospital ship which ferried Canadian wounded to Halifax, Nova Scotia. The ship was torpedoed by the Germans on June 27, 1918, and sunk off the coast of Ireland. MacLean and thirteen other nursing sisters on board died. She has no known grave.

CHARLOTTETOWN'S FINEST, N.D. This photo shows the view from the Government House entrance, and across Government Pond. It is easy to see a delightful Victorian city taking shape. Most of these homes overlooking the waterfront are still among the city's finest residences. Beaconsfield, home of the Prince Edward Island Heritage and Museum Association, is the building on the left.

FORT EDWARD AND THE DOGS OF WAR, N.D.

Although Charlottetown never experienced much in the way of military aggression, the possibility was recognized. The town remembered the American privateers who had raided the tiny settlement in 1775, pillaging the town, stealing the colony's official seal, and kidnapping the governor. After that incident a battery was built near Great George Street for defence of the town. In 1805 the Prince Edward Battery was relocated to Fort Edward in Victoria Park to provide further defence of the harbour from the threat of American privateers or Fenian raiders, for many felt attack to be imminent. Although never called on for any defensive action, six cannons guarded the city from potential invaders, and signalled important events. Gunners stationed at Ford Edward won numerous national artillery awards in the late 1800s and the early 1900s. The Dominion Artillery Association Trophy was awarded to the No. 1 Company, PEI Battalion, in 1894, a very prestigious and important test of military skill. For the artillerymen competing in this competition, perfecting their marksmanship skills was not only a matter of pride but a matter of necessity.

This early photograph shows the militia drilling between the battery and Government House. The size of the bridge over Government Pond, in the background, is proof of how the area has changed. This area has been used for military parades, celebrations, and even school processions. Although part of heavily used Victoria Park, the battery was neglected until recently. As part of Charlottetown's 150th celebration, the block house (where ammunition was stored), cannon (which had been brought from Fort Amherst across the harbour), and earthworks have all been restored.

Land surveying in a new territory was always taken seriously. To assure the accuracy of the surveying equipment a meridional line was established in Victoria Park in 1820. The three granite stones and a cannon barrel used for this purpose can still be seen at the Battery in Victoria Park which was recommissioned in 2005.

OUTINGS FROM THE CITY, N.D.

In 1865 the idea to appropriate up to half the property set aside for the lieutenant-governor for the enjoyment of the public came to light. Although the governors of the day were a little apprehensive at the idea of people wandering about so close to Government House, the idea became reality in 1873. The lands were "vested in the City of Charlottetown for the sole purpose of a Park, a Promenade and Pleasure grounds for…all her majesty's subjects." In Queen Victoria's jubilee year the roadway around the park was completed.

Victoria Park has had its moments. When men were spotted swimming in the nude, an act to prevent such actions was put in place in 1855. The park has seen many other recreational activities come and go. Over the years a toboggan slide was built, as were tennis courts, cricket fields, bathing facilities, ball fields, a swimming pool, and several lovers' lanes. The park has always been popular for walking, cycling, and picnicking.

AN AFTERNOON AT VICTORIA PARK, c.1910

By 1910 Charlottetown was the subject of many postcards lauding the charms of the city for tourists. This one, part of the "Garden of the Gulf" series, depicts the joys of relaxing on a park bench while enjoying the view of the harbour. The photograph was taken by W. S. Louson.

Chapter 3

Transportation — From Here to There and Back Again

NO EASY CROSSING, C.1906

These iceboats were about seventeen feet long, four feet wide, and were shaped to push the ice away. Sails, oars, and paddles were used to propel the boats through the water. The boats also had runners on both sides of the keel to make them slide easily over any ice and snow. They had long leather straps attached by chains along each gunwale. The other end of the strap was fitted with a harness and placed over the shoulders and around the waists of the crew and male passengers. Travellers paid two dollars for the trip if they assisted in pulling Her Majesty's mail. For double fare passengers could sit in the boat and do nothing. Ladies were taken across for double fare. Iceboats were the only means of winter transportation to and from the mainland until 1874, although they continued until at least 1906 when this photo was taken.

As Charlottetown grew, it became an important seaport with a bustling waterfront. Several wharves were built out into the harbour to provide the depth needed for visiting vessels. The lure of year-round crossing to the mainland soon became a priority and was one of the factors that led to PEI's decision to join Canada in 1873.

EARLY ICEBREAKER STANLEY, C.1900 The S.S. *Stanley* was one of PEI's early icebreakers, small in both size and power. In the winter of 1903 the ship drifted up and down the Northumberland Strait for sixty-six days, caught in an icepan.

When PEI joined the Dominion of Canada on July 1, 1873, the federal government promised continued services across Northumberland Strait. The first boat, S.S. *Albert*, was followed by S.S. *Northern Light*, Canada's first icebreaker. They were later replaced by S.S. *Minto* and S.S. *Stanley*.

ICEBREAKER *PRINCE EDWARD ISLAND*, C.1915

Work began on a year-round ferry service from Port Borden with an agreement in 1902. In 1915 the huge construction project became an attraction, with special excursion trains for those wishing to see the work being done. Since the needed pier was not ready in February 1916 when the S.S. *Prince Edward Island* arrived from England, the ferry was put into service between Charlottetown and Pictou, but did not carry railway cars. The service was moved to run between Port Borden and Cape Tormentine, New Brunswick, on October 15, 1917, carrying, among other things, rail cars filled with potatoes.

Pictured is the S.S. *Prince Edward Island* in Charlottetown Harbour while running the Pictou–Charlottetown route around 1915. With the age of motor travel came the need for an extra ferry, so in 1931 the palatial icebreaker S.S. *Charlottetown* came on the route. The Atlantic Ocean claimed the ship in 1941 when it hit a rock and sank off the coast on Nova Scotia on the way for a mechanical overhaul. Although more than fifty years old, the veteran *Prince Edward Island* maintained the link across the strait alone during the busy war years until the *Abegweit* started crossings in 1947.

HARTLAND CONNECTS COMMUNITIES, c.1930

The S.S. *Hartland* operated in local waters, making regular calls at wharves up the East River at Halliday's (Eldon), Brush Wharf (Orwell), and China Point in Orwell Bay; up the West River to Westville and the old West River Bridge; and up the strait to Victoria. The *Hartland* also ran chartered trips, particularly Sunday school picnic excursions. The service terminated about 1934.

ONE OF HOCHELAGA'S LAST RUNS, C.1940

S.S. *Hochelaga*, on the Charlottetown–Pictou route from the mid-1920s to 1940, is seen leaving the narrows of Charlottetown Harbour and moving into the Northumberland Strait. The ship left Charlottetown daily at 4:00 pm and arrived in Pictou at about 8:00 pm. It was due back in Charlottetown at 1:00 pm the following day. Passengers, cargo, and a few automobiles—loaded on by derrick—were carried on board.

PLYING THE HILLSBOROUGH, N.D.

The Hillsborough River has always served as a major transportation route. Roads parallel to the river connected the various rural communities, all of which were within short distance of a wharf. During the shipbuilding era more than five hundred vessels were built along the Hillsborough, contributing greatly to the city's economy. So important was the Hillsborough, that it was named a Canadian heritage river, the first of two in Prince Edward Island to receive such recognition. But one of the major challenges the river presented was, quite simply, crossing it—vital if travelling to the southeastern part of the Island.

Pictured is the ferry *Hillsborough*, named for the river it crossed. One could travel by boat from Charlottetown to Murphy's Point, which became Southport, and is now called Stratford. The first "ferry" was actually a large rowboat which was later replaced by a "team boat," named for the way it was moved by a team of horses who powered a paddle wheel by walking round and round the deck to turn a winch. This type of vessel was used until a steam ferry was introduced. For fifty years the ferry service was carried on by the *Ino*, *Ora*, *Hillsborough*, and *Elfin*, until the demands of traffic, which eventually included automobiles, determined that a bridge was needed.

WAITING FOR THE FERRY, C.1910

This horse and buggy patiently await the arrival of the ferry at the ferry wharf in Southport. Undoubtedly the driver enjoys the view of the city across the harbour. The ferry can be seen at the dock (in the centre of the photo) on the Charlottetown side. Although a bridge had been completed in 1905, in the beginning it was for train traffic only.

A bridge had been considered from Charlottetown as early as 1871 when surveyors were choosing a route for a proposed railroad but it wasn't until 1899 that the government passed the necessary Hillsborough Bridge bill. A contract was signed in 1900 with Toronto contractor M. J. Hanley Company, who brought machinery from the Crow's Nest Railway in the Rocky Mountains and from Montreal, as well as the superstructure, originally an Intercontinental Bridge no longer adequate for the traffic, from the Miramichi River in New Brunswick.

APPROACHES UNDER CONSTRUCTION, c.1901

Construction began first on the approaches. This required building temporary tracks to a field near St. Dunstan's College (now the University of Prince Edward Island) where a steam shovel loaded up an estimated fifteen to twenty thousand railway cars of clay. A train then brought the material to the bridge site, where a plow device pushed it off where it was needed.

Hillsborough Bridge Under Construction, c.1903

The Hillsborough Bridge was a great step forward as it provided continuous communication with eastern communities. The last span of the bridge was placed October 16, 1905. On October 23, 1905, the first train passed across the bridge, transporting a group of passengers en route to see Lieutenant-Governor MacKinnon. On the 26th the first train to cross the bridge directly out of Charlottetown went to Murray Harbour and back. Dr. George F. Dewar was the first to cross the bridge with horse and wagon. The bridge featured a swinging portion that opened to allow boat traffic to pass through.

New Bridge Replaces Old, c.1958

The old Hillsborough Bridge sees its last days in service as the newer bridge takes shape beside it. Railway tracks had been removed once trains no longer used this route. The pylons from the old bridge still stand today and are home to terns, cormorants, and other seabirds. This photograph is taken from the Stratford side of the Hillsborough River.

Snow Shovellers, c.1916

With trains came snow shovellers. Even with huge plows on the front, mighty train engines were no match for Mother Nature and often had to be rescued by man and shovel. After a major storm it was an honest day's work to be out digging a path for the trains.

Railway freight service began in late 1874 with an agreement to haul full carloads of grain until the close of navigation (shipping) each year due to winter. The railway officially opened in January of 1875, but the first trains sent out got struck in snowbanks. Snow continued to be a significant problem for the railroad for many years. Nevertheless, moving freight—and eventually, passengers—quickly became a way of life.

First Train, n.d. The locomotive shown here is one of the earliest used. The front stack indicates that it had been used as a wood burner. William L. C. Robinson was lieutenant-governor when PEI joined Confederation and when the Island's railway began service. He was the last governor to receive his appointment directly from the British Crown.

Excursion trains that began running within two months of the opening of the railway quickly became popular. The first "public" excursion saw the Methodist Sabbath School of Charlottetown taken to Morell for what was advertised as the "Grand Railway Picnic" in June 1875. Galbraith's Band was on board, and tickets were one dollar. Similar excursions brought Islanders together in towns all along the rail lines for grand picnics, hockey games, concerts, teas, basket picnics, evangelists, funerals, festivals, and all manner of entertainment. Even businesses used excursion trains to bring people into the city for sales. Rail excursions were very important social occasions and brought Islanders together as nothing had before. In 1889, a provincial tea necessitated the addition of six cars to the regular train in order to accommodate all the passengers. The coaches were so full that on the last leg of the trip, the train had to bypass several stops as there were no places left.

Sometimes, especially after events where liquor or competitive sports were a focus, the return voyage would get rowdy and require enforcement of law and order. Even so, excursions became so popular that the railways began requesting a certificate of attendance in order for passengers to get their trip home. For one excursion to a public address in May of 1890, the Women's Christian Temperance Union in Charlottetown announced that they would only issue the certificates for the free trip home at the end of the speech.

Harvest Excursions provided great opportunity for Islanders to see the rest of Canada—at least as far as the prairies—until well into the twentieth century. Tickets for farm labourers were just fourteen dollars each. A certificate came into play: labourers had to have them filled in by farmers they worked for, stating that they had worked for at least thirty days.

ALL ABOARD!
c.1910

The train is in at the second city train station. When Charlottetown opened its first terminal station in 1875, the local newspaper said it was elegantly furnished and had a two-hundred-foot platform. By 1898 it was condemned and thought to be in such bad condition that it was causing typhoid fever in workers. A new stone station was opened in 1907 after a pond was filled in so that tracks could be laid to it. Anyone referring to the city's early maps will see how the trains changed the waterfront. This station building still stands although the tracks are gone. It houses the Worker's Compensation Board and is easily seen on the waterfront.

OVERVIEW OF THE RAILWAY, C.1927

This aerial view of Charlottetown's waterfront clearly shows the rail yard and three rail lines leading to the station (top of photo). The round circle is the turntable, which allowed trains coming into Charlottetown to be turned to leave on the same tracks. Buildings beside the turntable were used to build railcars and perform maintenance. The top wharf shown was the railway wharf, where goods were transferred on and off seagoing vessels.

In 1905 fire totally destroyed much of the rail yard. A complete set of car shops were rebuilt, all brick to lessen the risk of fire in the future. New freight sheds were built in the location of the old station along with a new car shed, a new erecting shop, a new store, a new paint shop, and a new roundhouse. All manner of rail cars were built in the Charlottetown Car Shops—passenger coaches, postal cars, snowplows, baggage cars. (The most unusual car, built in 1902, was a six-deck affair with slatted sides, designed to carry live geese.)

In their rare spare time, the men at the railway shops built several new bridges out of old rails and material around the shop. The original railway was narrow gauge and since practically every mainland railway had switched to standard gauge, the shops became a manufacturer of boxcars, platform cars, passenger cars, and baggage and smoking cars. To become compatible with mainland trains and cars, the railway was gradually standardized in sections. In the beginning this meant adding a third rail outside of the narrow gauge, changing the wheels on cars and locomotives, and widening cuts and embankments to take the wider cars. The days of having to transfer goods from narrow gauge cars to those compatible with the rest of Canada ended in 1930. As well as rebuilding and refurbishing existing equipment, everything but locomotives was built there. These shops now house Founder's Hall, an interactive museum about the Fathers of Confederation, and a Visitor's Information Centre as part of the Charlottetown waterfront development.

CHARLOTTETOWN WATERFRONT, c.1900

This photograph, obviously taken as citizens and sailors prepared for some festivities on the waterfront, shows how the railroad was an integral part of life in Charlottetown. From this vantage point, looking up Great George Street, freight cars can clearly be seen on tracks that served the docks. This was a dramatic change in the short period of time since the Fathers of Confederation walked up this same street to Province House.

ROYALS VISIT, c.1951

Hon. T. W. L. Prowse meets Princess Elizabeth and her husband, Prince Philip, as they arrive in Charlottetown by train. Rail traffic across Hillsborough Bridge ended that same year, and trains were dispatched along an alternate route.

Rail traffic in PEI continued until December 28, 1989, when the last train was loaded onto the ferry, *John Hamilton Grey*. One wonders who among those in Borden to bid farewell to the trains knew that before too much longer the ferry would also sail from Borden for the last time.

WHOA NELLIE!
N.D.

The horse was the mode of transportation for over a century of Charlottetown's existence, and a whole industry of livery stables, carriage builders, and horse breeders, buyers, and sellers existed. This conveyance, identified simply as a "school bus," was surely a grand way to search out an education.

Crossed Keys Tavern was home to Charlottetown's first schoolhouse, and the proprietor divided his time and talents, as circumstances warranted, between his two dispensaries. Children were expected to pay the schoolmaster a substantial fee and contribute to his supply of tallow candles and firewood. The church was also a site for early education. There is reference to Sunday school at St. Paul's (Church of England) teaching the "three R's in connection with the fundamental truths of Christianity," which was followed by a free school begun at St. Paul's in 1823. The National School, established in 1820, required parents to pay for their children's education. In 1843 the *Colonial Herald* reported a building, again at St. Paul's, opened as an Infant School with an enrollment of 120 "scholars." Five years later, the Bog School (Anglican) was established for "coloured and whites of the poorer class, who were not only educated but reformed to the benefit of the whole neighbourhood."

LARGE'S LIVERY, c.1900 This street scene, at the corner of Queen and Kent streets in old Charlottetown, shows the vicinity of Large's Livery Stables. The high-wheeled sulky was standard equipment until the early 1900s and was used in the early days of harness racing.

Canada's first automobile, c.1859

You might say it was an instant love affair when Islanders and automobiles met. Of course there were those who saw autos as nuisances, polluting the air with noise and fumes. Farmers with horses had legitimate concerns. In fact, in 1913, the law was that only a few cars could be driven in a week, so that farmers knew it was safe to go to town with their horses. On market days, certain roads were forbidden to automobiles completely.

Pictured is a steam-driven car designed by Rev. Fr. Belcourt of Rustico and built to his specifications by a foundry in Pittsburgh in 1859. The car was shipped to Charlottetown in sections and assembled by White's Carriage Shop on King Square. On its arrival the steam car was demonstrated at picnics. Sometime later, while going down a long hill in South Rustico, the brakes failed and the car was wrecked. It therefore has the distinction of being not only the first automobile in Canada, but also the star performer in Canada's first automobile accident.

ADVENTUROUS TRAVEL TO BEACH PICNIC, C.1907

Pictured is the second automobile on Prince Edward Island. It was owned by a syndicate of Charlottetown men. One of the early tour companies, or taxi services, the auto was used to take passengers to Victoria Park and back for the sum of ten cents each.

First Gasoline Auto in PEI, c.1905

This Model A Ford, vintage 1903, is a tonneau back model with the rear section bolted onto the wooden body. This was the first production year for the Ford, which identified its cars with letters through to model T. This car was owned by George Auld and J. A. S. Bayer, a well-known Charlottetown photographer pictured here with his family. They purchased the car from T. B. Grady and Frank MacMillan of Summerside in 1904.

Although enthusiasts loved their autos, all was not well in the community. Agitation against the motor car—a result of the noise, frightened horses, and narrow and rough roads—grew with petitions and letters flooding the offices of politicians. There was great concern about the expenses needed to create or widen and maintain roads, and to supply gasoline and licenses. One suggestion was that automobiles be banned permanently to keep this nuisance from Island roads.

In 1908 the Automobile Act was passed, providing against the use of any motor vehicle on any public highway or street in the province. A motor vehicle was defined as all motors, automobiles, or vehicles propelled by any power other than muscular power except steam road rollers and such vehicles as run only on rails. The penalty for an infraction was a fine of five hundred dollars or six months in jail. Auto enthusiasts fought for change, and in 1913 the act was repealed, allowing the operation of motor vehicles three days a week—Monday, Wednesday, and Thursday—on the streets of Charlottetown. When war broke out, little attention was paid to the law and by 1919 a new Automobile Act was in force, bringing an end to the troubles faced by owners and operators.

In 1942 the government of Canada, as part of its war measures, imposed the rationing of gasoline. The system, as regulated by the Department of Munitions and Supply, required owners of motor vehicles to obtain a license to purchase gasoline and also issued owners ration coupon books. Each vehicle had a category and class designation, which determined how much gasoline would be allocated to it. The category was determined by how essential the vehicle owner's occupation was, and the class was designated by the make and model of the car. A rural veterinary surgeon (category C), for example, with a DeSoto (class 2), was allotted a maximum of 188 units (940 gallons) of gasoline per year.

People Carriers, c.1950 Buses started to run about 1937 from Charlottetown to Summerside and Borden, and to Tyne Valley and Tignish. In 1951 SMT took over from the Johnstons. Marvin Johnston had the run to Montague and Floyd Johnston had the run to Murray River.

"Red Devil" Wows the Crowds, c.1912

The first plane to fly over Charlottetown, in 1912, sparked an interest in flight among daring young men. Captain Tom Baldwin, an American, was brought to the Island by local businessmen, who initiated a public subscription to defray expenses. The "Red Devil" flying machine arrived by train, as Northumberland Strait would have presented too great an obstacle in an era when cross-country flight was in its infancy. The Red Devil thrilled patrons at the Provincial Exhibition in Charlottetown. Crowds took to the rooftops, and those who didn't have tickets peered through knotholes in the fence at what was, after all, an amazing event—humans in flight!

Regular flight was delayed in coming to the Island by the First World War, although some Islanders did learn to fly during the war years. An unofficial mail run from Truro arrived at the Exhibition Grounds in 1919. In the late 1920s Canadian Airlines Limited was granted a license to transport mail between Charlottetown and Moncton, landing ski-equipped aircraft on the ice off Victoria Park.

AERIAL VIEW, c.1925

With the coming of airplanes came an aerial view of the capital. This view shows the Hillsborough River to the right, the racetrack at the Provincial Exhibition Grounds in the upper centre, an active waterfront with several wharfs, including the railway wharf, at the top, and finally in the lower right corner, Victoria Park and Government House bordered by a large Government Pond.

"Puss Moth" Takes to the Air, c.1932

The first woman to obtain her pilot's license in Prince Edward Island, Mrs. Louise Jenkins, is shown with her own plane, "Puss Moth," at Upton Airport.

By 1931 Dr. Jack and Louise Jenkins made property available for the Upton Airport. The Jenkins property was used as the airport until construction of the more spacious aerodrome, which was built to meet the military needs of World War II. So enthusiastic were those "hooked" by this new mode of travel that the airport, although rather modest in size, quickly became a bustling place. Delivery of the mail quickly became a mainstay of this new method of transportation.

FIRST TO WED IN THE AIR, C.1934

The headlines read "Maritime Provinces Have First Wedding In The Air." In this photo the wedding party (left to right) is Walter Fowler, pilot; Rev. J. G. Wakeling; Margaret Littlewood, bride; Russel Lent, groom; and Walter S. Grant, witness.

**AVIATOR HERO
CARL BURKE
BUILDS AIRLINE,
c.1946**

When Carl Burke was a boy in Charlottetown, he dreamed of being a pilot. Flying lessons were expensive in the 1930s, costing ten dollars an hour, and the nearest flying school was in Saint John. When he started to work in Charlottetown for twelve dollars a week, he saved every penny for flying lessons. When he finally became a pilot he saved again to buy a small second-hand airplane. Travellers, especially those with important business on the mainland who missed the train ferry, would call Carl. With a sandwich in his pocket, he would meet them during his noon hour and fly them over for fifty dollars. During World War II he became a transatlantic ferry pilot flying warplanes made in Canada to Great Britain. During this time he and fellow ferry pilot, Joseph Anderson, made plans to start an airline serving New Brunswick, Nova Scotia, Prince Edward Island, the Magdalene Islands and St. Pierre and Miquelon. On his final trip for the overseas ferry service, Anderson crashed his plane and died. Burke carried on and opened Maritime Central Airways, or MCA as it became known in 1941. He served the region well and was acknowledged for remarkable work in transportation development in Labrador and the Arctic. Burke was made an officer of the order of the British Empire by King George VI for his dangerous rescue of four RCAF fliers whose plane had been forced down on a patch of drifting ice in the Gulf of St. Lawrence. They radioed for assistance but the RCAF planes were too large to land on the ice and provide assistance. Burke flew to Moncton where a two-seater plane was equipped with skis. He took the men to shore one at a time, performing the difficult landing four times. This photo shows Captain C. F. Burke on the right at the inaugural flight of Maritime Central Airways to Nova Scotia.

FLYERS BRING THRILLS, N.D.

As important as Upton Airport and its aircraft were for transportation, mail delivery, and missions of mercy, there was still time to thrill the crowds, and probably offer up some challenges for local daredevils who joined the competitions.

Chapter 4

Commerce and Agriculture

MR. AND MRS. JAMES PEAKE, JR., C.1879

At one time there were fine shipyards along the Charlottetown waterfront. The fine trees that grew down to the waterline were a valuable resource that provided the timber for boat building, one of the Island's earliest exports. During the "Golden Age of Sail," between 1830 and 1880, shipbuilding was the chief industry in the Maritime provinces. From the Duncan shipyard, the largest ship ever built on the Island was launched in 1858 and christened the *Ethel*. The three-deck, 1,795 ton ship was sold in England. From the Peake shipyard came the *Fanny*, built by James Peake. The ship was bought in 1849 by a group of Islanders who wanted to go to California, where gold had been discovered. They sailed around the Horn to San Francisco in six months, sold the *Fanny*, and set off for the gold fields.

Shipbuilder, merchant, and leading businessman James Peake, Jr., built an enduring symbol of Victorian elegance, which he named Beaconsfield, in the late 1870s. It was said to be a visible expression of Peake's social and economic standing in the community. Even so, the Peakes were destined to enjoy their creation for just over five years. A lingering recession and the collapse of the Island's shipbuilding industry spelled ruin for James Peake. He lost his fortune and in 1882 sold the home.

Two factors led to the decline of shipbuilding in Charlottetown: the introduction of iron ships and the sad fact that most of the Island's forest had been cut down. Poverty replaced plenty for men who made a good living building ships and now found themselves out of work. The same era saw the loss of the carriage-building industry. The loss of these important industries contributed to a great many men leaving to find work in other places.

BEACONSFIELD, ENDURING SYMBOL OF VICTORIAN ELEGANCE, C.1930

This photograph of Beaconsfield taken from the northwest corner shows gardens as well as architectural details of the house and porches. Designed by architect William Critchlow Harris, the twenty-five-room home was well equipped with all the latest conveniences, including gas lighting and a form of central heating. With eight fireplaces and imported chandeliers, one of Charlottetown's finest homes was fit for royalty. When the Marquis of Lorne (Governor General of Canada) and Princess Louise (daughter of Queen Victoria) visited Charlottetown in 1879, Mrs. Peake's father, T. H. Haviland, the lieutenant-governor, entertained the regal party at dinner at Beaconsfield. It served as the Cundall residence from 1883 to 1916, and sometime between 1916 and 1936 it was a YWCA residence. Today, Beaconsfield Historic House, located near Government House and Victoria Park on Kent Street, is home to the Prince Edward Island Museum and Heritage Foundation.

Last Coal Boat, c.1930s

After these longshoremen unloaded the last coal boat in Charlottetown, they took time out to pose for a photo. Note the horses and wagons in the rear used for delivering coal. Moving from coal to alternate sources of heat would have surely made for a better environment in the city.

ELLIS DISTILLERY, N.D.

To bring the "taste of the Highlands" to Prince Edward Island, this distillery was brought over from Scotland in 1847 by Mr. Ellis, grandfather of William Ellis in Sherwood. It was displayed in the family grocery store.

One of Charlottetown's less-reputable commercial enterprises was that of bootlegging. Plebiscites held in Charlottetown in the late 1800s saw the drys win, then lose a later vote to the wets. By 1892 Charlottetown had roughly seventy-five liquor outlets. But by 1901 PEI had the distinction of becoming the first province to successfully enact a prohibition statute. It was a huge political issue and was one of the first times that women exerted their political power. Temperance societies, where women were known to be passionately vocal, drove politicians to take steps designed to keep the population sober. The sale of alcohol was banned except for medicinal, industrial, and sacramental uses—loopholes which the temperance folk battled constantly for the following few decades.

Despite temperance efforts, and the law on paper, bootlegger operations flourished with brisk sales of illegal moonshine and imported liquor and wine. It is a commonly known, but seldom-documented fact that fortunes were made through the illegal production, importation, and sale of liquor. There are few, if any photos of the "industry," since most bootleggers had to operate under a curtain of secrecy. By the 1920s, most of the whiskey, wines, and rum was picked up on the French islands of Saint Pierre and Miquelon (off the coast of Newfoundland) and landed on PEI's north shore. The liquor was then smuggled over land to Charlottetown, where bootleggers could fetch a fair price.

Prince Edward Island's prohibition era ended with the Temperance Act of 1948. Government liquor stores opened, but the sale of liquor was still tightly controlled, with taverns and bars forbidden until the mid-1960s. It was an atmosphere that led to home brews being concocted in stills hidden away from prying eyes. Often referred to as "mother's milk," the homemade liquor was usually fiery and potent. The fact that it was not until 1948 that alcohol could be purchased legally surprised many people. It certainly surprised the fly boys who came to PEI for training during World War II.

BEACH GROVE INN, c.1925

The tourist trade was quickly acknowledged as being an important source of revenue for a province that had much to offer: sunshine, scenery, good fishing, good food, and a bit of an adventure to get there. Travel to Charlottetown was by ship or train, followed by horse and buggy. When the Automobile Act was passed in 1908, banning all automobiles, it cost the province several million dollars in lost tourism revenue. In 1913 autos were allowed to operate three days a week, but it was not until 1919 that tourists could come to Charlottetown knowing they could drive without fear of a five-hundred-dollar fine, or of being arrested and sent to jail. Considering that the wealthy—those who could afford to travel to Charlottetown for a vacation—were turning from trains and steamboats to their own motorized transportation, the move to finally allow cars was a good, if contentious, idea.

One of Charlottetown's grand old hotels, Beach Grove Inn, was built on the North River in 1921 by R. H. Sterns of Souris. Sterns had previously operated the Victoria Hotel in Charlottetown. In its heyday the resort offered tennis courts, beautiful lawns, a driveway, a nine-hole golf course, and could accommodate 125 guests. Its guest list was indicative of the increasing potential of tourism. In its second year of operation, Beach Grove welcomed sixty-five guests from many American cities, including Honolulu, and from as far away as New Zealand. Although Beach Grove's life as a resort was relatively short, the building and grounds continue to service Islanders today. In the fall of 1939, just four years after Sterns's death, the PEI military began using it as training headquarters. Later it was used as accommodation for inmates of the overcrowded provincial infirmary. In 1946 the 120-acre estate was purchased by the provincial government and made into a seniors' home. Today the area is the site of Beach Grove Home, a new building housing a seniors' residence, forestry district office, a commemmorative forest, and nature trails.

The Charlottetown, c.1945

The establishment of grand hotels in the twentieth century became one of the most visible signs of growth in the tourism industry. In 1931 the opening of a new Canadian national hotel was described by the newspaper as "a red letter week in the social life and marks an era of progress in this Province." As part of the railway hotel system, there were great expectations of an "increased influx of traffic that would fill all of the hotels in PEI." This photo, of "Bunny" Chapman was taken in front of the hotel now known as the Charlottetown, on Kent Street.

Charlottetown Wharf, n.d.

Farming implements on a Charlottetown wharf symbolize the link between farmers, seafarers, and the city economy. The implements demonstrate how far agriculture had come from the days when early farmers used crude one-furrow plows guided by a single handle. It wasn't until around 1810 that the two-handle plows were introduced. Grain was cut with scythes and sickles, and threshed by hand. In 1828 the first threshing machines arrived, driven by a horse-powered treadmill.

With the exception of the St. Lawrence River Valley, Prince Edward Island has the oldest continuous history of agriculture in the country. Agriculture has been part of Charlottetown's heritage and economy from the days when every home had space for livestock and gardens to grow their own food. The city market became a vital outlet for selling goods, and the city's wharves took Island products to the world. Service industries and suppliers to agriculture became part of the city economy. Agricultural research and education have played important roles in the city that continue to this day.

EXPERIMENTAL FARM, C.1917

A stately but dilapidated ten-room mansion called Ravenwood (also known as the Pope property) became home to the Charlottetown Experimental Station and Farm, which has operated at the original site since 1909. It has served every imaginable facet of the agricultural industry with research and development. Located in the heart of the city, it was a strong link between rural and urban Islanders for social occasions as well as for commerce. The grounds were often used for picnics and other outdoor events. Weather observation was also conducted at the farm, and although the service has, over the decades, continued, the methods of, and parameters for, collecting weather information have become increasingly complex. Over 1,300 persons attended the demonstration of potato spraying machinery at the experimental farm that is pictured here.

PEI Pottery operated between 1800 and 1900 at the site now owned by the experimental farm, north of Lily Pond. There were originally three ponds on the property to obtain clay for pottery and brickmaking. Two were later filled in and a third converted to a lily pond thanks to the foresight of one Dr. William Saunders. He obtained the lily plants from a dealer in Kentucky in 1910. The root stalks were established and, after a few problems with insects, the plants began to thrive, attracting countless visitors to the farm. By 1920, the pond was completely covered with lily leaves and blooms. To this day, the pond fills with blossoms, a tribute to the keen perception of Dr. Saunders.

Providing plant research, c.1916

When the Woolners of Rustico came to PEI they brought with them seeds of an English barley named Chevalier. It was grown for a number of years and became known as Old Island Two-Row. This barley was separated into several distinct types at the experimental station. One of these strains was called Charlottetown #80 and was licensed in 1916. The outstanding feature of this barley that commended it to farmers was its habit of dropping its awns in the field, thus aiding in clean threshing.

EXHIBITION BUILDING, N.D.

In the early years these grounds were the site of many activities, with the highlights of the year being the provincial agricultural exhibition, which featured tented booths and a midway, and harness racing. By the 1880s the Island could boast of more than two dozen harness racing tracks. The Charlottetown Driving Park, the star of them all, opened its doors for standardbred harness racing in 1889 and began attracting enthusiasts from around the world.

Fire Strikes Exhibition, c.1945

The beautiful main building on the Charlottetown Exhibition Grounds, near the Hillsborough River, was erected in 1890 and was a landmark in the city for more than half a century. The spacious, well-appointed building was destroyed in a spectacular fire in April 1945. The coliseum opened in 1952 and took the place of this building.

A RACE DAY ON THE HALF-MILE TRACK OF THE CHARLOTTETOWN DRIVING PARK ASSOCIATION, CHARLOTTETOWN.

CHARLOTTETOWN DRIVING PARK GRANDSTAND, N.D. Race day on the half-mile track of the Charlottetown Driving Park Association drew crowds of harness racing enthusiasts. This stately grandstand was built in 1889 and formally opened in 1890. Double-tiered, the wooden stand had a capacity for more than 3,000, and at times an overflow crowd of some 5,000 for a big race. The upper deck of the stand was removed in later years and the lower deck remained in use until it was destroyed by fire in 1961. The judge's stand to the right is now a national historic site. Notice the large wheels on the sulkies. These everyday carriages were forerunners to modern sulkies.

OLD HOME WEEK, 1942

A stage set trackside during Old Home Week featured a variety of acts including the American Eagles highwire act and a bicycle-riding bear.

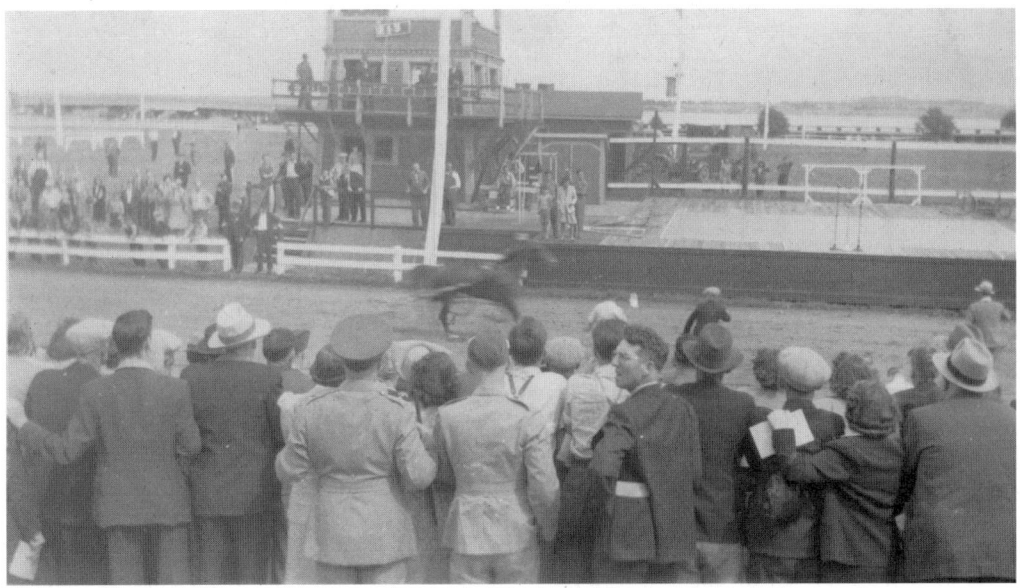

SOLDIER FROM WAR ZONE TAKES IN OLD HOME WEEK, C.1942

When Russell Bowes of Dorchester, New Brunswick, visited Old Home Week in 1942, he captured moments from the Provincial Exhibition. Bowes, who served his country in World War II, visited the Island when on leave from the Royal Canadian Air Force. This entry finished the mile in 2:22:25—driverless.

FREE-FOR-ALLERS FIRST GOLD CUP AND SAUCER RACE, C.1961

Each August, during Old Home Week and the provincial exhibition, the Charlottetown Driving Park hosts the Gold Cup and Saucer Race. The fastest horses and the best drivers in all of eastern Canada converge for fifteen racing programs in nine days. The Gold Cup and Saucer, dating back to the early 1960s, has become known as an especially prestigious horse race. Pictured are the starters for the first Gold Cup and Saucer Race in 1961. The event has grown into one of the biggest sporting attractions of the year in PEI.

Horses were important for more than harness racing, though. Before the automobile, horses were not only necessary for transportation, working the fields, and making deliveries—even powering the ferry across the Hillsborough River—but as status symbols and important parts of celebration. The breeding, caring for, supplying for, and buying and selling of horses were the basis for many businesses. One fine horse, Roncesvalles, a thoroughbred of the best blood from England, was brought to PEI to improve the local horse breeding. He died in 1838, but not before leaving very fine progeny behind him.

The Parkman family of horses was founded by a thoroughbred mare brought to the Island in 1838 from Devon, England. The Parkmans predominantly bred pure- and mixed-blood horses—hackney, thoroughbred, standardbred, and French Canadian—and acquired animals off-Island to breed with local stock. Breeding was carried out with both beauty and practicality in mind, and the progeny have mostly been saddle or carriage horses. Most of the animals were sold off-Island, in the Maritimes, Ontario, Quebec, and in pre-automobile days, Bermuda. Parkman mares were also bred to Saint Sylvestre and he is apparently responsible for much of the grey stock, and the particularly thoroughbred air and carriage that was long visible in the province.

Equine Elegance on Parade, c.1912

Showy horses were often seen in Charlottetown for state visits and other special occasions. This beautiful pair were used during the visit to Prince Edward Island by Governor General Duke of Connaught and the Duchess. The barouche is shown leaving Government House, driving the vice-regal party past the Cundall Home.

SAINT SYLVESTRE, c.1935

Saint Sylvestre, thoroughbred stallion, was 16.2 hands tall and weighed 1450 pounds. Born 1924 in His Majesty's King George's stables, he raced in England, where he was the winner of the Saint Leger, and was imported to Canada with the Canadian Light Horse Society. He was well known in Toronto for having produced some outstanding colts with nice disposition and good size. Shown at the Royal Winter Fair, Saint Sylvestre was grand champion thoroughbred stallion and reserve grand champion a second time. Some of his offspring were also champions.

From 1925 to 1948, Mr. and Mrs. Raoul Reymond owned and operated a fox farm. They acquired two thoroughbred mares and began looking for a stallion. Walter Shaw, then provincial minister of agriculture, was on the lookout for a good prospect. He went to Ontario and contacted Hughie Wilson, coach of Canada's equestrian team, who was apparently fed up with the horse business and consented to sell Saint Sylvestre. Horse enthusiasts in Ontario were outraged, judging the horse would be completely wasted in PEI. Without him the Island at that time would have had nothing in the way of thoroughbred breeding stock. He was said to have single-handedly influenced local stock. His contribution to PEI's horse lineage would have been even greater had the Reymonds not bought back many of his better offspring, and had there been more knowledge in the community of how best to breed him.

The Reymonds also bred standardbreds, were regular exhibitors in all classes at the provincial exhibition, and were among the founding members of the Crowlands Riding Club, to which they supplied hounds (English foxhounds and American walker hounds) for the local hunts. They presented twelve dogs to the club, replacing these with another twelve when the first lot was killed off by some mouldy dog biscuits. Mrs. Reymond also sent a litter to Mrs. Churchill Mann, and these animals formed the basis of the pack for the Ottawa hunt. The Crowlands Riding Club was founded in 1933 or 1934 with Haligonian Dick Zwicker the sometimes riding instructor. The club organized afternoons of riding, leaving from the Bayfied–Duvar residence on North River Road. It was disbanded in 1939 with the outbreak of war.

CHARLOTTETOWN'S COAT OF ARMS

CITY OF CHARLOTTETOWN

So important was the silver fox industry to Prince Edward Island, a silver fox appears in the coat of arms for the province. In the late 1800s the rare silver fox was native to the region, and its pelt was highly prized in many parts of the world. It was in Prince Edward Island that the art and science of breeding fur-bearing animals was developed and refined, and the ranched fur industry born. Fur farming made a tremendous contribution to the early twentieth century economy, and the skill and knowledge of the industry's Island pioneers, as well as the superior quality of their product, was appreciated worldwide. While the heart of silver fox farming was in western PEI, Charlottetown was certainly part of the industry as well. Breeders, the Canada fox exchange, fox shows, and sales were all located in the capital.

The superb quality and uniqueness of the silver fox industry attracted even royalty. HRH Edward Prince of Wales visited the Woodman Ranch at Spring Park (in Charlottetown).

GEORGE ROBEY, PRINCE OF A FOX, c.1929

J. P. Hooper of Charlottetown is shown with his silver fox, George Robey. The silver fox industry turned many Islanders into rich men. In 1916 Prince Edward Island fox pelts sold by the sales board of the Silver Black Fox Breeders Association of PEI for an average price of $912.50 per pelt.

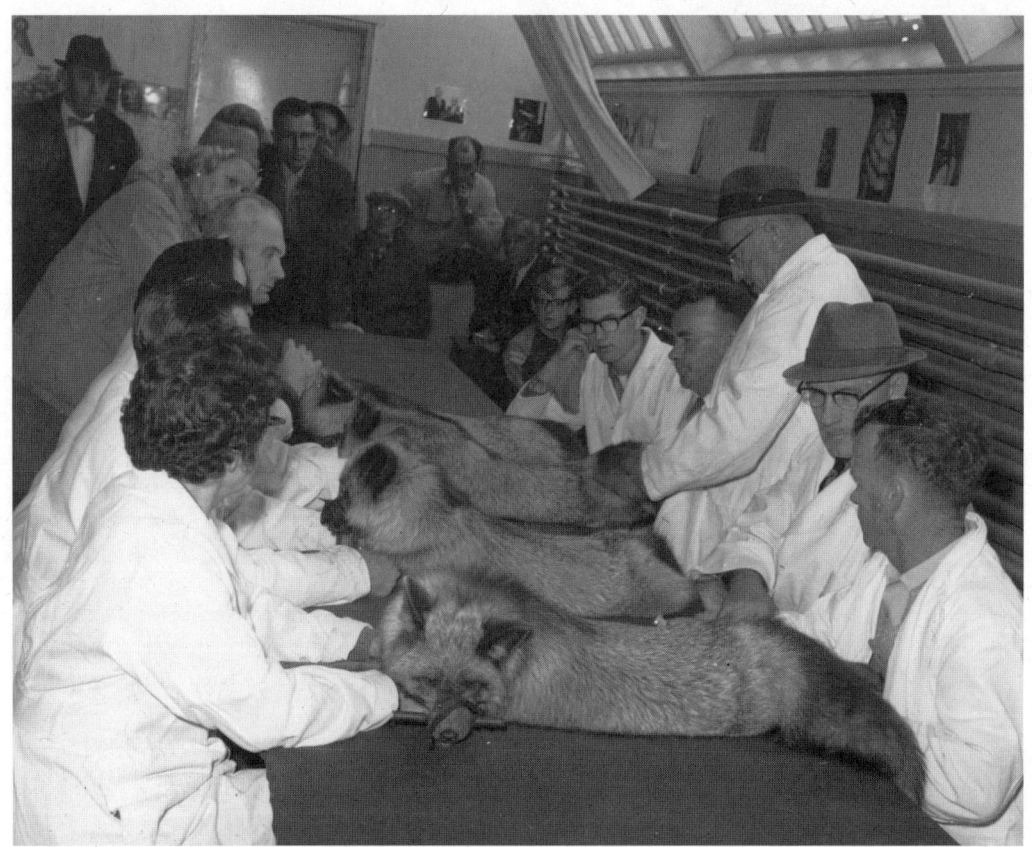

FOX AND MINK SHOW, C.1966 Even after the silver fox industry slumped, breeding enthusiasts continued to hold the annual Fox and Mink Show in Charlottetown each November. Judging was "live pelt," meaning that the live animal was judged as breeding stock, rather than as a pelt. This event was unique and continues to attract ranchers, as well as buyers, from far and near.

Chapter 5

Culture and Community

TO BE OR NOT TO BE? C.1885

This question must surely have been asked by these members of the first Shakespeare Club formed in Charlottetown. They certainly look as if studying the works of the playwright was a serious business indeed.

TOUCH OF THE BLARNEY GRACES CITY STAGE, c.1894

The Charlottetown Benevolent Irish Society, the oldest national society in Prince Edward Island, is a branch of the Benevolent Irish Society founded in April 1825 by John Ready, then lieutenant-governor of the colony. The traditional St. Patrick's Day play has been an annual affair sponsored by the BIS. Shown here is the cast of the play *Robert Emmett*, produced at the Lyceum Theatre, March 17, 1894.

Masonic Lodge Opera House, c.1894

The finest and most elegant of Charlottetown theatres, the Masonic Lodge Opera House, located on Grafton Street just west of Queen, was built in 1891 by architects Phillips and Chappell. The first performance was *A Russian Honeymoon*. The three-storey building sat one thousand people in the first-floor theatre. The St. John's and Victoria Lodge Mason groups met in the upper theatres. With the advent of motion pictures, the opera house was transformed into the Prince Edward Island Theatre and around 1913, followed the Wonderland at the Market House putting this new medium on its screens. In later years there was a confection store at the southeast corner of the building—undoubtedly so that folks could take a stash of sweet treats in to watch their movie. The theatre was destroyed by fire on December 14, 1955.

DRUMMING UP AN AUDIENCE, C.1900 When travelling shows or special productions came into town they would take to the streets to drum up an audience. This crowd gathered to see the promoters of a minstrel show at the corner of Queen and Grafton streets.

LOTS OF LAUGHS, c.1900

All forms of live performance were popular, including a laugh or two at the zany antics of the policemen from the stage production of *Pirates of Penzance*. Live theatre was part of the Island social scene for many years and in 1932 a royal charter established the Dominion Drama Festival. Just a short time later, in 1935, the Little Theatre Guild of Charlottetown was established and began staging plays that were performed locally. Regional adjudications chose which performance groups would go on to the final Dominion-wide competition. Both the drama festival and the theatre guild went into hiatus through the war years, although the guild continued to give benefit performances and "Carry on Canada" concerts for the armed services stationed in Charlottetown. The guild reorganized in 1946–1947, introducing children's plays in 1949–1950. The guild gradually diminished after the Confederation Centre of the Arts opened in 1964.

NATHANIEL STROMBERG, c.1890

When Professor Nathaniel Stromberg called his son, John, for his music lessons, he probably never dreamed just how far music would take him. An accomplished musician in his own right, Nathaniel conducted a boy's band in Charlottetown for many years. He also taught school as a young man.

CHARLOTTETOWN TO BROADWAY, C.1895

John Stromberg (1853–1902), photographed with his orchestra, was part of Broadway's early history. His music is cited as the turning point of the musical shows of the 1890s, paving the way for later composers like Irving Berlin and Richard Rogers. Before 1895, revues were a mixture of the minstrel show and comedian, but when the Weber and Fields company, with their Canadian composer, moved into Broadway, stage boxes sold for one thousand dollars each.

Still sung and recorded today, compositions by John Stromberg were written for the Weber and Fields show on Broadway entitled *Fiddle-Dee-Dee*. Starring the three top musical performers of the Gay Nineties—Lillian Russell, Fay Tempelton, and DeWolf Hopper—it was a burlesque on the presentation, *Quo Vadis*. It later became available on Decca records with Al Jolson and his orchestra. Recordings were also made by Maurice Chevalier and Bing Crosby.

CHARLOTTETOWN'S FIRST BRASS BAND—THE LEAGUE OF CROSS BAND, C.1905

This brass band was often enjoyed during holiday festivities, at local dance halls, at church picnics, and in parades. The band was a group formed by the Catholic Church. In their matching peaked hats, stand-up collar jackets, and shiny black shoes, they presented a professional image suitable for the best of events. Several of the musicians were also members of the 105th Battalion Band.

BANDS ON PARADE, N.D.

The militia held parades and manoeuvres on public holidays. Torchlight processions and displays of fireworks were part of many community celebrations, particularly the Queen's birthday and visits by important dignitaries. Bands were an important part of community life, as their musicians led parades, played at dances and concerts, and livened up bazaars, suppers, and picnics. Bands not only played a good variety of tunes with diverse instruments and talent, but also sometimes decked themselves out in colourful uniforms, to the delight of audiences.

DON MESSER'S ISLANDERS, c.1948

In 1939 Don Messer and his Islanders went coast to coast for the first time, broadcasting from Charlottetown's CFCY radio station. They became some of Canada's most beloved performers. This photograph show Don Messer (left) fiddling, with Marg Osburne and Charlie Chamberlain at the microphone.

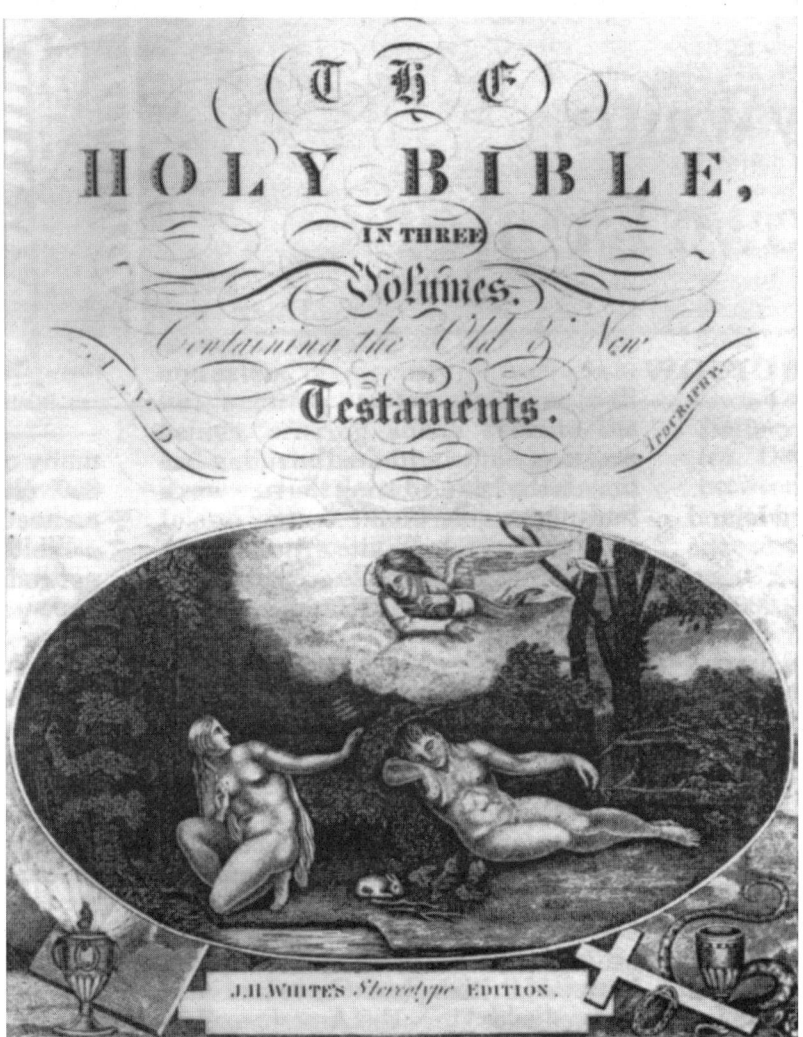

CANADA'S FIRST BIBLE, C.1832

In 1832, John Henry White, a Charlottetown printer, produced a two-volume edition of the Bible containing seventeen lithograph illustrations. It is believed to be the first Bible ever printed in what is now Canada.

"Get the News,"
c.1900

With the coming of newspapers, came jobs for young boys hawking the news around town. These newspaper boys are offering up the *Daily Examiner*. The *Examiner* began as a weekly in 1847 and became the Island's first daily newspaper in 1877.

The newspaper has been an import communication tool since 1787, with at least one being printed every year since, with only a few exceptions or lapses in publication. At least twenty-six different newspapers have been published in Charlottetown. The current daily, the *Guardian*, first put ink to paper in 1890. The large number of daily and weekly newspapers that flourished in the nineteenth and early twentieth century were "vital instruments in the development of colonial public opinion and the consequent enrichment of colonial life," wrote Frank MacKinnon in *Charlottetown Centennial 1855-1955*.

LUCY MAUD MONTGOMERY, PEI'S MOST FAMOUS DAUGHTER, C.1890

It was the same Charlottetown newspaper that gave Lucy Maud Montgomery, PEI's most famous author, her first rejection as a writer, and three years later her first published credit. Her first published work, a 156-line poem about the murder of Captain LeForce titled "On Cape Leforce" was written in 1890, just before her sixteenth birthday. In 1891 she wrote another piece based on Island lore and legend, an essay "The Wreck of the Marco Polo," which was again published in the *Patriot*. At sixteen young Montgomery was already becoming a well-known writer. By 1893 she decided to become a schoolteacher so that she could support herself while pursuing her writing career. To do so, she left her home in Cavendish to further her education in Charlottetown. Although only twenty-four miles away, the move to the "city" seemed to signal great change. When Montgomery went to Prince of Wales College, in 1893, the population of the capital was only 11,000 but this was the capital—the biggest town, the province's chief port and market centre. Electric street lights had just been installed and must have presented a beautiful image where they shined on the waters of the harbour. She was happy as a college girl in Charlottetown and loved the friendships and learning in spite of the spartan life of her boarding house. It was after she made the move that she was published in the *Ladies World*, a popular magazine that actually paid for her work, granted only with a magazine subscription.

Toward the end of her time in Charlottetown, Montgomery gave a lecture of her composition of Portia, heroine of Shakespeare's *Merchant of Venice*, at the Charlottetown Opera House. In spite of a plumped-up face from a toothache and a bad case of stage fright, she received praise for the presentation, with the *Charlottetown Guardian* asking permission to print her essay. Her writing career led to the publishing of nearly 300 short stories, over 250 poems, some 20 novels, and countless articles. Lucy Maud Montgomery's work will never be forgotten in Charlottetown, where her most beloved novel, *Anne Of Green Gables*, was developed into a musical production, which is now the longest-running Canadian musical, playing each summer season at the Confederation Centre of the Arts. In 1908 Maud was asked to write the words to a hymn about Prince Edward Island after dignitaries realized that the province didn't have an official song. It wasn't until March 1909 that music was composed to go with her words, and the Island hymn was performed to the public for the first time at the Opera House. Maud herself didn't hear her hymn performed until 1929, when she gave a talk at the institute in Mayfield.

ROBERT HARRIS, N.D.

If Lucy Maud captured the essence of Prince Edward Island with her pen, then artist Robert Harris deserves equal credit for capturing it with his paintbrush. Born in Wales, Robert Harris and his family arrived on the island in 1856. He was raised on Prince Edward Island, received his first training in Boston, and then studied art in London and Paris before becoming a renowned illustrator and portrait painter. When he returned to Canada, he settled in Toronto, then the principal art centre in the country, although he returned to PEI often. Harris was known not only for his portraits, but also for his images of life on PEI. He painted many small landscapes and scenes of the colonial experience in a narrative style called genre painting. Using this style, which was very popular in the mid-1800s in the United States and Europe, painters such as Harris explored the Canadian landscape around them for subjects. He recorded places and painted the people of PEI at work and at play.

FATHERS OF CONFEDERATION, c.1865

There are many interesting tales associated with the 1864 Charlottetown Conference. A young musician of Welsh parentage was among those at the banquet and ball that were the climax of the week. Twenty years later, that young man, then recognized as an accomplished portrait painter—was commissioned to paint what was to become one of Canada's best known pieces of art: *The Fathers of Confederation*. That painter, Robert Harris, and his brother, William Critchlow Harris, not only recorded history, but left a wonderful legacy of architecture and imagery which we treasure to this day. It is to be certain that when the barque *Isabel* unloaded its passengers onto a Charlottetown pier in 1856, no one present had any idea that this new family, the Harrises, would leave such a distinct mark on the city, and indeed on Canada.

LADY MARGARET BANNERMAN, N.D.

When Lady Margaret Bannerman set foot on Prince Edward Island, she was returning to the scene of her youth. Granddaughter of Walter Patterson, she was best known as "Carlyle's first love," possibly referring to a liaison with writer Thomas Carlyle. A woman of the world, Lady Margaret was described as tall, stately, and a most gracious hostess who filled the position of Governor's wife to perfection—even if her image seems a little flamboyant today. She had married Sir Alexander Bannerman, a Scot, who came to the Island in 1850 when he was appointed lieutenant-governor. Bannerman was credited with instituting responsible government on PEI. Their stay was short—in 1854 Bannerman was appointed governor of the Bahamas, and in 1858 governor of Newfoundland.

**LEFT:
HELEN BAYFIELD,
C.1862**

The essence of Charlottetown in the 1860s—the era of Confederation—was captured by talented women artists like Helen Bayfield (pictured here), Fanny (Wright) Bayfield, and Mary Caroline Bayfield. Helen and her mother Fanny were known to be particularly artistic, and did much to record Charlottetown as it was in their lifetime. As well as passing along artistic expression to their family, Helen (1839–1867) and Fanny taught painting and music to the ladies of Charlottetown. Helen was also an assistant to well-known photographer Henry Cundall and helped ensure his work a place in history. Helen herself was also interested in photography, and probably experimented in the process. Much of her personal collection of over three hundred photographs is now preserved.

**RIGHT:
HENRY CUNDALL,
C. LATE 1800S**

By profession, Henry Cundall (1833–1916) was a surveyor as well as a land and business agent. His legacy, however, comes more from his talents as an amateur photographer. He began capturing images of Charlottetown when he acquired a "photographic apparatus" in 1859. Thankfully for today's researchers, Cundall also kept diaries of his photographic work which provide insight into life in early Prince Edward Island and around the Maritimes, England, and Scotland, where he frequently travelled. He shared his joy of the captured image by purchasing photographic images to supplement his own and enlightened delighted audiences through what were known as "magic lantern shows."

LATE NINETEENTH-CENTURY FASHION, c.1880

Fashion changed dramatically in the time period covered by this book and it was a matter of pride for Charlottetonians to be seen as up to date. Fortunately early fashion was slow to change, because news of what was stylish and what was not had to come by sailing ship, and often through word of mouth. With printing presses, the advent of newspapers and catalogues made the fashionable more accessible.

Men were not to be left out of the fashion scene. In the 1880s trousers had no creases or turn-ups, and side moustaches and whiskers were worn. Notice how small the lapels and collar of the jacket were. Trousers in the late nineties began to develop a vertical crease and turn-ups.

OUTING AT THE BEACH, C.1890

This unidentified group of fun-loving beachgoers clearly demonstrate that many types of bathing suits existed around 1890. Short sleeves were typical, but knee-length trousers with a skirt on top were all the rage. Dark colours with braid and lace decorations were normal. On the right, a sterner group of full-clothed ladies, many protecting their fair skin from the sun with umbrellas, are apparently chaperoning the younger group.

CLOTHING THE PEOPLE, C.1876

While talk of fashion may seem frivolous, providing clothing and footwear was an important contributor to the economy. Bootmakers and tailors, such as these shown on Victoria Row (now Richmond Street), were important retail businesses. Entrepreneurs, their employees, suppliers, and distributors are the foundation of the city's economy.

PICNICS WITH STYLE, C.1913

Picnics like this one were a common sight at the Experimental Farm for many years as farmers' groups, women's institutes, and schoolchildren held picnics there during the summer months. This photo shows a group of farmers from Cornwall ready for their meal.

In the summer, great portions of the population turned out for the numerous fairs, teas, excursions, sailing regattas, and even carnivals that were held, for instance, in Market Square with rides and refreshment booths. Sunday schools and societies held big outdoor events, often at Kensington Pasture, now the Exhibition Grounds. Picnics were popular among Island church groups and fraternal societies. An 1864 Benevolent Irish Society outing to Warren Farm was typical. The steamer *Heather Belle* was hired to ferry the group to Rocky Point, where violinists and a college band provided entertainment.

FASHIONABLE NUPTIALS, C.1925

The first world war had a dramatic impact on fashion in Prince Edward Island. First of all the frills and flamboyance of the Victorian era was set aside for a more down to business face of reality. Clothing became more subdued. Secondly, fabric was not as plentiful, a fact that probably a perfect excuse to make clothing more comfortable and more functional. These fashion trends are readily apparent in this typical 1920s home wedding photo. The wedding united C. N. Bissett and A. Peake.

POST-WAR FASHION, C.1925

By 1922, after the war, dresses were slimmer and shorter than before. With its huge destruction of young men, the war had a dramatic affect on a society that found the glorification of the boyish ideal reflected in fashion. The waistline was lowered and the skirts were almost to the knee. The day costume preserved a neat businesslike simplicity. Hair was worn close to the head and shingled.

Chapter 6

Sporting Affairs

PENNY FARTHINGS, N.D.

The bicycle was popular in Charlottetown, whether for sheer pleasure like that enjoyed by this group trying out the unique two-wheeler known as a "penny-farthing," or in competitive bicycle racing.

PRINCELY CRICKETERS, 1919

When the Prince of Wales visited Charlottetown in 1919 he took time out to meet with a group of Charlottetown cricketers in Victoria Park. Prince George is the seventh from the right in the picture, wearing a grey hat and black tie and has a cigarette in his hand. He would become King George. Records show that cricket was played widely in the nineteenth century, and remained very popular into the 1900s. In the nineteenth and early twentieth century a number of prominent business and professional men, generally referred to locally as "sports," were dedicated to recreation. Through their efforts Charlottetown established cricket and tennis clubs, sleighing clubs, rowing and boating clubs, golf, and hockey. The Victoria era saw the formalization of many sports that had been enjoyed by citizens for years. Many associations or institutions started in Victorian times have endured to this day.

One of the most important single events in Charlottetown's athletic history was the founding of the YMCA in 1863. Brigadier W. W. Reid wrote that this building was the first of its kind to open in North American. Other important events in Charlottetown's sporting history included the opening of the first indoor skating rink in 1872. The Prince Edward Island Rifle Association was formed in 1875, and produced many famous shots over the years. The first official game of lacrosse was played on the grounds of the Government House in 1877 and the first lawn tennis match in the same place in 1883.

Tennis Popularity Included the Ladies of the Town, c.1911

When eleven men met in 1889 and decided to form the Charlottetown Lawn Tennis Club, it was not the first of its kind in the city. The MicMac Lawn Tennis Club and the Fitzroy Tennis Club, already in existence, were invited to join the new club. The Fitzroy group consented to join on the condition that the constitution be amended so as to admit ladies as full members rather than as associate members, which permitted them a voice in the club's business.

Sporting Affairs 121

PULL TOGETHER BOYS, C.1920

Members of the Hillsborough Boating Club are shown taking a break in training at the Ferry Wharf, in 1920. In its day the Hillsborough Rowing Club was a very popular summer activity. The railroad shops can be seen in the background of this photo, at the bottom of Prince Street. Water sports in Charlottetown Harbour and the three rivers that feed it were very popular. One of the city's first automobiles offered "excursions" to Victoria Park. Swimming from the Victoria Park beach, and also from one near what is now Beachgrove Home, helped while away hot summer days.

THE CHARLOTTETOWN YACHT CLUB HOUSE, C.1939

The old Hillsborough Boat Club took on the moniker the Charlottetown Yacht Club and continues the tradition of keeping boating and water sports alive in the city today. The yacht club was formed in 1936, and had its first active season in 1937. Fred Morris was its first commodore. Many members of the RAF belonged to the yacht club during World War Two when in Charlottetown for training.

ALWAYS READY FOR A DARE, C.1936

This sporting young miss was captured aquaplaning in Charlottetown Harbour.

FIRST CANADIAN SWIMMING AND WATER SAFETY INSTRUCTIONAL SCHOOL, C.1945

Evelyn Cudmore became a volunteer member of the Red Cross Corps in 1939. In 1945, she attended the first national conference on water safety and became director of this program. Upon her return, she immediately started to organize the first Water Safety Instructor's School in Canada. There were almost one hundred pupils enrolled in that year; in the next, ten thousand enrolled in the program. She received from Lord Mountbatten the Distinguished Service Award of the Royal Lifesaving Society. She is shown at the far right, with the Prince Edward Island division of the Swimming and Water Safety Instructor School at the Charlottetown Yacht Club.

FORE! C.1928

In 1893 there were reports that Charlottetown golfers played in Saint John, New Brunswick. By 1903 Dodd & Rogers, one of the city's leading hardware stores, was advertising golf equipment. Somewhere in-between, two Charlottetown golf clubs were formed: the Charlottetown Golf Club and the Belvidere Golf Club (later spelled "Belvedere") operated side-by-side for a number of years.

In their wonderful book, *A Treasure Called Belvedere*, Ron H. Atkinson, W. A. Bill Beer, and Harry K. Simmonds document in great detail just how golf came to Charlottetown. In 1902 the decision was made to form a club. Until a location for a golf course could be found, they were welcomed by the Provincial Exhibition Association to set up a few holes on the racetrack infield at the exhibition grounds. The judge's stand served as a temporary clubhouse. Golfers placed a few markers, buried some tomato cans, and laid out a small seven-hole course. Since the infield was also used to pasture horses, there was some congestion to deal with, but enthusiasts persevered.

A mandate to find a home that was easily accessible by horse and buggy was set along with club dues: a twelve-dollar entrance fee for gentlemen and five dollars for ladies with a two-dollar annual fee. An organizing committee soon entered into a lease agreement for Alexander Beazeley's Belvidere Woods. The first nine holes opened in 1903, an amazing feat considering the lack of heavy equipment available at the time. The first course was rough: cattle and sheep were used to keep the fairway grass down and greens were fenced to keep the livestock off the putting areas.

Soon, Belvidere Golf Club (sometimes called Belvidere Links) was considered one of the most outstanding courses in eastern Canada. Other details from its history provide a window onto life in the city. In 1905, there were sixty-two lady members compared to fifty-six men. When Europe went to war in 1914, golfers felt the effects. Not only did many male members depart to fight overseas, but times were so difficult, and supplies so hard to get, that many Maritime golf courses closed until the war was over. The Charlottetown Golf Club stayed open to provide a site for citizens to relax and try to forget the trauma friends and families were going through across the sea. Golf balls were in very short supply because of the war effort's need for rubber. Caddying became an important job for city youth. By the late 1930s a "caddymaster" organized them and a caddy's "union" ensured their fair treatment. As it was a good walk or bike ride from the city to the links, a pickup point for caddies and golfers, by the power pole at the corner of Victory and Longworth avenues, became known as "Caddy Corner."

When the winds of war swept Europe in 1937, there was increased activity at the PEI Lighthorse Shooting Range at Kensington Point, just across from the seventh fairway. In the interest of safety, the seventh, eighth, and ninth fairways were closed during active shooting periods. With the second world war membership decreased, but those left home enthusiastically carried on. The club invited officers of the Royal Air Force Navigation School at Maple Hill to golf. Because the men were very transient, special mess golf memberships were arranged and many of the young visiting airmen made good use of them. The war had a noticeable negative effect on the fairways at Belvidere, as lime and fertilizer became impossible to obtain.

Dashing Through the Snow, c.1840

One of the most popular winter activities among young people revolved around horses and sleighs. Pleasure outings and racing on the frozen harbour, or on marked-off sections of town streets, would be followed by a skating party, a dance with supper, or a basket social. The Charlottetown Sleighing Club and the Tandem Club were both popular. Speaking about the Tandem Club, one observer wrote of "a procession of sleighs driven tandem by the officers and young men of the town. The bright trappings of the horses, the merry jingle of the bells, and the bright colourings of the ladies' costumes, along with the comfortable sleigh robes, make a pretty picture long to be remembered."

DOWNHILL SLIDING, C.1893

Tobogganing was long a popular winter activity. Since Charlottetown didn't have much in the way of suitable hills, the citizens built their own. This one, photographed in Victoria Park in 1893 by Arthur Johnson, was just one of several built in the capital over the years. It had been built in 1870 and was accessible to members of the Victoria Toboggan Club, who maintained and regulated its use. In 1886 the club declared that smoking on the slide was prohibited in the presence of ladies. In 1905 members of the Charlottetown Golf Club built a giant toboggan slide beside the clubhouse to provide a little fun for members' families. Similar to the one shown in this photograph, it was said that proper icing of the boards could result in a good rate of speed, taking sledders as far as three hundred yards. The slide was so popular with the citizens that the club began charging for its use. Ultimately, the work involved and the wear and tear on the clubhouse were more than the fledgling golf club wanted, so they dismantled the slide. For the next few years there was a large toboggan slide erected each winter at the Edward Bayfield estate on North River Road (Victoria Park area) in the west end of the city. It is not known if it was the same structure.

CHARLOTTETOWN
ABBIES, C.1898

Hockey has long been a vital part of Island life, not only because of the teams that have brought glory to Charlottetown, but also as a game played out in backyard ice patches and streets of the city. The Abegweit (or Abbies as they are known locally) and Victoria hockey teams were Maritime champions well-known across the country. Sport rivalry between Charlottetown and Summerside in the 1920s and 1930s particularly, resulted in many exciting moments. So popular was hockey and so great the rivalry that special trains loaded with "Red Hot Rooters" followed the Charlottetown Abegweits when the game was in Summerside. Summerside fans came back in equally large numbers when games were in Charlottetown. Competition flourished and reached a peak in 1931. The rivalry between the two groups of fans was so heated that the final game for the Prince Edward Island championship was played in Moncton, as it was felt unsafe to hold the game in either of the teams' hometowns. Summerside won that game, but the next year Charlottetown, along with a number of other Maritime centres, joined a major hockey league. The rivalry, which had begun two decades earlier, was never as intense again.

The name Abegweit was to become synonymous with good spectator sport. The Abegweit Athletic Club was the city's oldest and only incorporated athletic association and was still functioning more than one hundred years later promoting and directing amateur athletics. In 1886, after only two years of practice play, the Abegweit Club rugby team, representing the city's best athletes, won the Maritime title for the first time.

Interestingly, minor hockey did not formalize until 1948 when Bill Reid began to organize teams and games on the ponds of the city squares. Reid became known locally as the founder of minor hockey in Charlottetown. Under his enthusiastic leadership, minor hockey games moved into the Forum in 1954.

MICMAC HOCKEY CLUB, C.1903

Pictured is one of the first Charlottetown girls' hockey teams on record. Although there is no record of their performance, it is known that girls' teams also formed in Summerside in 1905, so they must have had some stiff competition.

ASPIRING TO THE NHL, C.1919

The Millionaires hockey team were certainly a debonair-looking group as they posed for this photo commemorating their win as amateur champions of the Maritime provinces.

UP AND OVER, c.1925

Wallie Scantlebury clears the pole vault at eleven feet during the track and field meet in Charlottetown. He was Maritime champion in 1925–26. Note the vaulter's cap is still on his head and the old rigid bamboo pole he is using. Scantlebury, a multi-faceted athlete, was also a bicycle racer—a big attraction at track and field meets from 1900-1930. This photo won a number of awards for action photography.

Chapter 7

In Service to Others

BISHOP MACEACHERN, C.1860

Angus Bernard MacEachern was born in 1759 at Kinlock Miodart, Scotland. When his parents came to what was then St. John's Island in 1772, Angus Bernard remained in Scotland to attend college. He studied philosophy and theology and was ordained into the priesthood in Spain in 1787. The young priest, saddened by colonists' letters and accounts of hardships, asked permission to go to America and arrived at St. John's Island in August 1790. Having been without a resident priest for so long, it is difficult to imagine the joy of the colonists meeting Father MacEachern. In 1819 he was appointed bishop of Prince Edward Island, New Brunswick, and Cape Breton, over which he exercised jurisdiction until his death in 1835. By that time, eighteen churches had been built. In winter, snowshoes and skates were Father MacEachern's constant companions.

In the early nineteenth century the only places of Catholic worship on Prince Edward Island were at Scotchfort and Malpeque. The log church of St. John's—

built at Scotchfort by the Highland immigrants who had come to the Island in 1772—had fallen into disrepair and was condemned as a place of worship by the bishop of Quebec. He instructed Father MacEachern to build a suitable church at St. Andrew's. Accordingly, MacEachern and his devoted congregation set about the task, and in 1804, completed the church, described by a visiting bishop as "elegant and well finished." The church served the people of St. Andrew's for almost sixty years. By 1860, the people had outgrown their church and a new one was built to serve the rising capacity. After its completion, the old church was transported on the ice by one hundred horses and five hundred men, Protestants and Catholics, to Charlottetown to be used as a school by the Sisters of Notre-Dame. This old church became the central section of Rochford Square School on Pownal Street. In modern times, after a fire destroyed part of the building, the old church was returned to St. Andrews where it is now a historic site.

ST. DUNSTAN'S CATHEDRAL, c.1849

The census of 1841 gave Charlottetown and Royalty a population of four thousand, of whom seventeen hundred were members of the Catholic church. The old St. Dunstan's Church, although much enlarged ten years previously, was much too small to accommodate the throngs that came to church every Sunday. In July of 1843, the cornerstone of the new building was laid by Bishop Bernard MacDonald. This was to be the cathedral, the mother church of the diocese. It was 140 feet long, and 70 feet wide. It stood on the west side of Great George, having its front on Dorchester Street, and was completed in 1848.

St. Dunstan's Burns, c.1913

A crowd gathered to watch in disbelief as St. Dunstan's Cathedral burned in 1913. Built of stone in 1907, this massive cathedral replaced a wooden cathedral built in 1843. The 1907 church was considered to be one of the most magnificent east of Quebec. It was rebuilt and opened again in 1919, with its status raised to that of a basilica ten years later.

St. James Presbyterian, c.1880

St. James Church, the first Presbyterian place of worship in Charlottetown, is one of the oldest Protestant churches in the city, being opened for worship in 1828. Its walls have witnessed the triumphs and successes of many of the town's citizens as well as one of its most endearing tales, the phantom bell ringers of St. James. The story has endured so long, and had so many credible witnesses, that it has become part of local lore.

On a melancholy fall day in 1853, one Captain Cross, who had risen with the sun, made his way from his home on Brighton Road to Royal Oak Stables to tend to a prize horse just arrived from Devon. He had almost reached Black Sam's Bridge when he heard, as he thought, a ship's bell—clear and distinct, eight bells coming not from the sea, but from the heart of town. He heard it again, and as he reached Pownal Street, again, now as a dreary toll. He made his way back to the entrance to Government House, noticed the *Fairy Queen* had not yet left for Pictou, and decided to investigate the bell, which was still tolling. His quest took him to St. James Church where he beheld, in the entryway, three women dressed in white with uncovered heads and feet. As he approached, the church doors closed on the women. Joined by Davy Nicholson, Kirk sexton, they decided to investigate and tried to enter the church. The door was securely fastened. The sexton made his way to the manse for a key while the captain stayed at the church, now aware that a gale had blown up, causing high winds to whip around the church. The sexton returned, accompanied by Kirk minister Dr. Snodgrass. The trio made their way inside and to the belfry. Nicholson and the captain both later claimed to see the women on the staircase. Unable to find anything further, they left the church to hear that others had heard the bell at the same hour. That afternoon it was learned that the mail steamer, *Fairy Queen*, had been lost in the strait. Seven passengers were lost, of whom three ladies were members of the St. James congregation. The captain and crew of the ship were later tried for dereliction of duty for abandoning their passengers. The publicity the trial generated made the phantom bell ringers a talked-about sensation for generations to come.

COLONEL LUTIE DESBRISAY, C.1930

Colonel DesBrisay, a great granddaughter of the rector of St. Paul's Church, was born in Charlottetown in 1868. Throughout an active career of sixty years, she was an outstanding member of the Salvation Army in Canada. She was elevated to staff rank at the age of twenty-one, an achievement never before attained by anyone in the army at such an early age. She served in Toronto for many years, inspecting and visiting army works in all parts of Canada, organizing the army work in Bermuda and other centres. She died in 1945 just a few days after making an address.

Town Constables, c.1830

Quality of life in Charlottetown improved significantly following the arrival of town constables. These police officers were quite distinctive in their long frock coats, high beaver hats with a black leather band, and red "billies," or clubs, hanging from a strap around their wrist. This photo shows the courthouse and town hall, along with the gas lights, which were the pride of the city.

The first criminal code came into effect in 1792 listing eleven crimes that warranted execution: treason, murder, attempted murder, manslaughter, concealing the death of an illegitimate child, the "detestable" sin of buggery, rape, breaking and entering during the day and taking away goods up to five shillings, armed robbery, arson, and extorting money. The first person sentenced to death in the colony was a servant, Elizabeth Mutely, whose crime was stealing just over seven pounds from her master. She was pardoned when no person was found who would execute a woman.

HARVEY'S BRIG, c.1832

Being a seaport was both a blessing and a curse for Charlottetown, for along with other goods came cheap West Indian rum, lots of it! Along with celebrations that ended in brawls, assault and robbery were not uncommon. Charlottetown relied first on local militia to keep order. Justice was present but rudimentary and penalties for crime were tough. Because early Charlottetown had no jail, criminals tended to get either a death sentence—even for simple robbery—or be set free. As punishment became more sophisticated, public lashings at a whipping post in Market Square became more common. Punishment could even include being tied to the back of a cart and lashed as it was driven through the streets. Criminals were also made to do hard labour and records show that the ground for the Colonial Building (now known as Province House) was levelled by a gang of criminals chained to a cart they hauled along. Those found guilty of a lesser crime would have been relieved when a small jail, known as "Harvey's Brig," was put up on Connaught Square (a.k.a. Pownal Square). Governor Ready laid the cornerstone for this jail in 1830, and it was used for over eighty years.

BIG DONALD'S FIRST HOME, C.1876

An exciting development was the arrival of a fire bell, which was first hung in the market building on Queen Square. In 1876 an extension was added to the building to provide space for a police station and a belfry to house a new fire bell. Prior to the fire bell, the residents had relied on the town crier to sound the alarm for a fire. The warning was passed by word of mouth as quickly as possible, but it was not a very efficient way to warn citizens or call in the volunteer firefighters. The bell was a great boon to the city. Known as "Big Donald," it was named after the fire chief of 1875, Donald MacKinnon. Notice the town water pump at the left end of the building. The water supply consisted of seven large underground water tanks and sixty-one pumps and wells in various parts of the city. This supply often proved unsatisfactory and firefighters sometimes had to resort to the Hillsborough River. In 1888, a system of waterworks was developed that placed eighty-eight fire hydrants in the city. From 1888 to 1916, the volunteer fire department was supplied with hand-drawn hose reels and two steam-powered fire engines. Firefighting was a serious business in the late nineteenth century—1877 city records show the various volunteer fire departments in Charlottetown counted 272 members.

CITY HALL SHOWS OFF FIRE EQUIPMENT, c.1890

With the construction of the new city hall in 1888, the eight subsidiary fire stations were concentrated in the new station, which took up the northwest end of the original building. The department's stables, with six stalls, opened onto Queen Street. Stalls were equipped with automatic doors so that when the fire alarm sounded, a bolt could be drawn and all doors would open simultaneously. The horses were then harnessed in the engine room. The new location greatly reduced the cost of maintenance. In 1916 an addition to city hall provided space for fire engines. City hall's tower, sixty-six feet high, was topped by a belfry to house "Big Donald," the fire bell, and was equipped with hooks which were used for hanging firehoses to dry. In September 1952 an air horn, which is still in use today, was installed for sounding fire alarms. In 1966 Big Donald was retired to its present location—on the lawn on the Kent Street side of city hall.

The earliest firefighting equipment in the capital was the bucket. Often made of leather, it was to be kept, filled with water, by the door of every home. Before the Charlottetown Fire Department was established in 1855, each household was expected to keep extra fire buckets for emergencies, man the bucket brigade, and help pump the hand pump and the hand-operated engine when they came into use. The steam engine arrived in the city as a direct result of one of the most serious crises in the history of Charlottetown. Early in the morning of July 15, 1866, a blaze started in a house near the corner of King and Pownal Streets, and a westerly wind drove it through the town to Great George Street. Nearly the entire town was out to help in the bucket brigade, but the conflagration was not brought under control until two hundred buildings were destroyed. "The Great Fire of 1866" destroyed over four city blocks. Spreading unchecked in a northeasterly direction, it destroyed all in its path until it reached Bishop's Palace, which was made of stone, and vacant ground on Great George Street.

CHARLOTTETOWN FIRE DEPARTMENT'S HOSE REEL TEAM, C.1925

Drills, competitions, and tests of fitness have long been part of the life of a firefighter. This team set a world record of 1:09 3/5 in the gruelling hose reel race in 1925, and won many other events across the Maritimes against other fire departments. Clockwise from left: Bob Allen, Neil (Tiny) Matheson, George Wood, Phil MacDonald, "Mac" MacLeod, W. Wood, Angus MacEachern (coach), Chief Ranahan, George Walker, W. Coyle, Louis Stewart, Jack Connelly, Allen Stewart, and John Turner, Jr.

St. Andrew's — Travelling School House, c.1880

Students and teachers are seen in front of St. Joseph's Convent on Pownal Street. This building, St. Andrew's Chapel, has a unique history. Scottish settlers who had arrived in 1772 had been without a church until 1805 when, under the direction of Father MacEachern, they built St. Andrew's. The first major church in Prince Edward Island, it served the Island until it was replaced by a larger church in 1862. After standing abandoned for two years, it was called into service again. The chapel, obviously well constructed by those early pioneers, was moved twenty miles over the ice to Charlottetown, an amazing feat for its day. First-hand accounts tell of five hundred men and fifty teams of horses, slowly dragging the building on runners down the Hillsborough River. All went well until they hit the thin ice close to the shore. When the chapel went through the ice into the mud, it made the final leg very difficult for man and beast. Even so, on the third day of the challenging journey, the chapel found its new home. It was renovated and given to the Sisters of Notre Dame, who opened it as St. Joseph's Convent School in 1864 with one hundred or so pupils. They continued operating the school for girls for more than a century. Damaged by fire in 1987, the building was cut into four pieces in 1998 and moved back to St. Andrew's near Mount Stewart, where it has become a historic site.

HIGHER LEARNING AT PRINCE OF WALES COLLEGE, c.1900

The Central Academy school, established in 1836, was renamed Prince of Wales College in 1860 to commemorate the visit of the Prince of Wales. Prince of Wales College was long known for having an excellent reputation as a Canadian educational institution. This photograph features the original Central Academy building and the Prince of Wales faculty of 1900. The building of the new Prince of Wales structure can be seen in the background. This new building was completed in 1900 under architect C. B. Chappell. The school opened as a junior college that offered the final two years of high school, the first two years of university, and a normal school for training teachers. The Normal School of Charlottetown had amalgamated with Prince of Wales College in 1879. In 1932, the Prince of Wales College building was destroyed by fire. Classes resumed two days later in the Queen Square and Prince Street School buildings until a new building opened in 1933. In 1965, Prince of Wales College was renamed as a university and in 1968–1969, Prince of Wales amalgamated with St. Dunstan's University to become what is now the University of Prince Edward Island. The Prince of Wales building is now part of Holland College.

PROTESTANT HOSPITAL BUILDING

The first Protestant Hospital in Prince Edward Island was built at Longworth Avenue at Cumberland Corner in Charlottetown. This building had a twelve-bed capacity, with an additional wing. In 1898 it was replaced with another hospital and became an apartment house. The second building was used until 1930, when a new hospital was built in Victoria Park on Brighton Road.

ST. BERTHE, c.1920

Rev. Sr. St. Berthe, Grey Nun, was the first superintendent of the Charlottetown Hospital School of Nursing, established in 1920. Disease was a significant problem in Charlottetown, as it was in many regions of Canada. In fact, Prince Edward Island in the 1920s had the highest rate of tuberculosis (TB), commonly known as consumption, in the country. Earlier in the 1880s a report estimated that one in five deaths in Charlottetown was caused by the disease. Treating it required ongoing care, education, specialized treatment, and hospital stays. While volunteer organizations did their best, they simply did not have enough money or time, and began to pressure the government to create permanent Departments of Health. In Prince Edward Island that happened in 1931. Within a generation, TB was almost eradicated. Other diseases that were a constant concern in the nineteenth and early twentieth century included: typhus, typhoid, diphtheria, and smallpox.

CHARLOTTETOWN HOSPITAL BUILDING

The first Roman Catholic Hospital in Prince Edward Island, located on Dorchester Street just west of St. Dunstan's Cathedral, opened in 1879 in the former residence of Bishop MacIntyre and had a capacity of twelve beds. The Grey Nuns of the Order of the Sisters of Charity from Quebec City came to Charlottetown to staff the hospital and aid the city's sick and poor. In 1885, a horrifying smallpox epidemic occurred, and a second house was acquired on the outskirts of the city. Soon there were one hundred smallpox patients, which the Grey Nuns nursed heroically. In about 1895 the first building was moved to the corner of Haviland and Dorchester streets and became an apartment house. The second Charlottetown Hospital, built in 1882 and enlarged in 1891, was partly destroyed by fire in 1921. It was repaired and again occupied until 1925, when a third hospital was completed. The second hospital became the Sacred Heart home for the aged and infirm until its demolition in 1963.

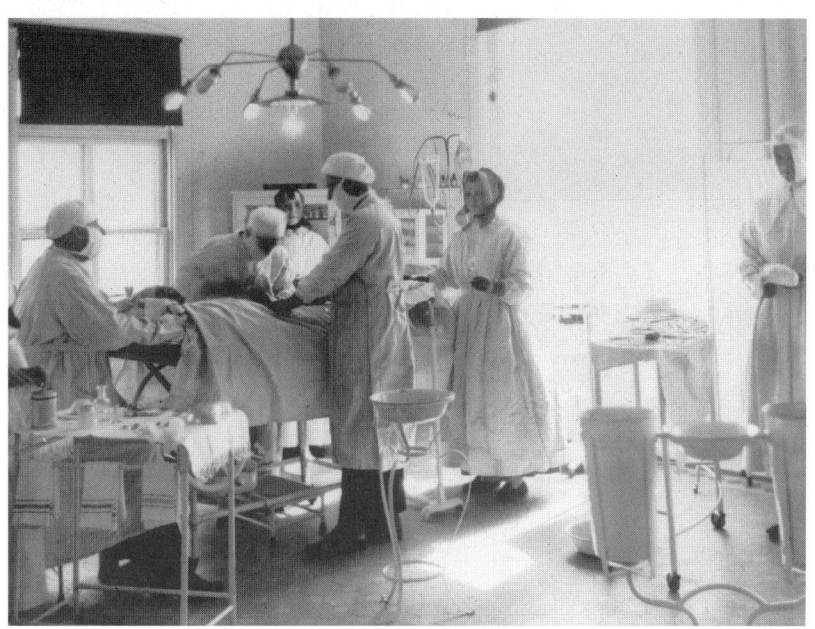

UNDER THE KNIFE, c.1915

An operating room in the old Charlottetown Hospital. Drs. S. R. Jenkins, J. O. McGuigan and W. J. P. MacMillan are the attending physicians, assisted by Grey Nuns.

WOMEN'S INSTITUTE CONVENTION, PRINCE OF WALES COLLEGE, C.1925

The first Women's Institute on the Island was organized at York in 1911. Two years later, institutes were organized under the Department of Agriculture and eventually grew to 265 branches, with a membership of four thousand carrying on a wide and varied program. One of their earliest projects was creating a provincial sanatorium to fight tuberculosis. It was largely due to the institute's efforts that the sanatorium was built in Charlottetown and the annex added. Not only did the Women's Institute effectively petition government to provide proper treatment for TB, it also came forward to raise the funds. The government had promised to contribute one third of the ninety-thousand-dollar estimated cost. By the end of their campaign, the Women's Institute had surpassed the amount of their promised funds with almost seventy-eight thousand dollars pledged by the end of 1929. The organization contributed in no small measure to the betterment and enrichment of community life. During the two world wars, Women's Institutes donated thousands of articles to the soldiers. Their other projects included: "The Handicraft Van," which visited various Institute chapters to encourage craft production, music and drama festivals, the PEI Exhibition, and home economics scholarships. The Women's Institute also presented briefs and resolutions to the provincial government recommending a residence for girls at Prince of Wales College and were happy to see this request granted with the opening of Montgomery Hall in 1961.

THE FIRST RED CROSS BLOOD DONOR TEAM, C.1948

Miss Iphigenie Arsenault, commissioner of the PEI division, greeted the first Red Cross blood donor team to come to Charlottetown. This Halifax team came five times yearly for clinics.

Formed during the first world war to support the war effort, the Red Cross Society became an important element in the health and welfare of Prince Edward Island, turning its programs to public health after the war. The Red Cross focused on disease prevention in rural as well as urban areas, and for many, the Red Cross was the first organization to show interest in their health. The Red Cross was, for example, involved in the battle against tuberculosis, and recognized the role of nutrition and hygiene in fighting the disease. Over the years, the organization's mandate broadened to include many different activities, including swimming lessons for youngsters, disaster relief, blood collection, and specialized treatment.

Children with disabilities were treated at semi-annual clinics organized by the Prince Edward Island Red Cross for thirty-five years, from 1926–1961. Until 1926 there were no interested organizations to offer such help.

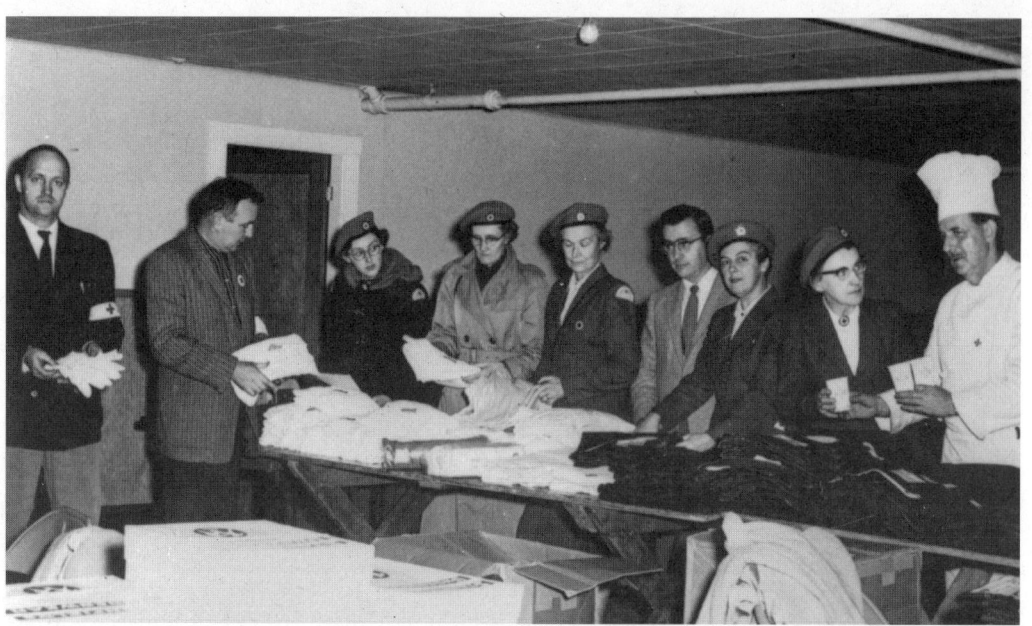

Disaster Team Ready to Roll, c.1956

The Red Cross disaster team is ready to leave for the Springhill mine disaster. In the 1950s, the town of Springhill, Nova Scotia, was devastated by two of the worst mining disasters in Canadian history. An explosion in 1956 killed thirty-nine miners, and another seventy-four died in the "bump" of 1958. PEI's Red Cross team was always ready to provide assistance when nearby communities faced a crisis.

Chapter 8

Answering the Call to Arms

MILITIA AT THE READY, N.D.

From the city's birth, the military or militia have had a presence in the capital. After American privateers raided "Charlotte Town" in 1776, thoughts turned to defending the town. In his original survey, Captain Samuel Holland noted two sites for defence. One became St. George's Battery and Barracks (near Water and Haviland streets) although the residents were ill-equipped for battle. The other would later become Fort Edward Battery in what is now Victoria Park. As part of the British effort to defend the Island, four "provincial companies" from Halifax arrived in Charlottetown in July 1778. Each year regiments were sent to PEI until war with Russia caused their withdrawal. Under the first Militia Act passed in 1780, all males between the ages of sixteen and sixty would bear arms and attend musters and military exercises. Fortunately the city was never attacked again, for the law was little observed, and musters that were held were looked upon as a joke, often amounting only to roll call and the enjoyment of a keg of beer. Even so, musters were part of life for a century.

Rumours of an intended invasion of Britain by France raised the martial spirit throughout the British Empire in 1860. On the Island, companies mustering upwards of one thousand men were furnished with arms and trained. Despite its continuing reputation as a social club, the militia did prove effective on the few occasions it was needed, such as fighting the Great Fire of 1866 and during the Belfast Riot.

RIFLEMEN ON TARGET, C.1889

The Prince Edward Island rifle team, winners of the Dominion of Canada telegraphic rifle match in 1889.

One competition riflemen, and later women, aspired to was held in England, and fondly referred to as "Bisley." Islanders did well at this prestigious event, which was founded in 1859 to provide a focus for marksmanship for the corps of volunteers raised to meet the perceived threat of invasion by the French. In 1894 the National Rifle Association was granted a royal charter that continues to this day for "promotion of marksmanship in the interests of the Defence of Realm and permanence of the Volunteer Forces, Navy, Military and Air."

The association organized the first set of competitions in 1860. Queen Victoria fired the first shot and gave a prize of £250 for the best individual marksman, setting the pattern for annual meetings held every year except during the world wars. The Queen's Prize remains the premier award and the July imperial meeting is internationally renowned. It was moved to Bisley, where the Princess of Wales, later Queen Alexandra, fired the first shot at the beginning of the 1890 imperial meeting.

GUN DRILL IN CHARLOTTETOWN, c.1890

Islanders have always been known as quick volunteers to fight for just cause. The Boer War was no exception and marked the first time a group of soldiers from the newly joined province went to war, as part of a Canadian contingent of about seven thousand. When Charlottetonians went off to war, the citizens turned out to ensure a good send-off. In 1899 when some thirty "brave fellows" boarded the train, the *Daily Examiner* reported "torpedoes cracked, whistles blew and the great crowd cheered. It was thought there were at least three thousand people in and about the railway station, and the streets along the line of march from the drill shed were well filled with spectators. As the contingent and military escort marched to the patriotic music furnished by the Artillery Band they were repeatedly cheered by the spectators and when they reached the railway station a grand ovation awaited them."

MILITIA AT THE READY, C.1900

Members of the 2nd Regiment Charlottetown Engineers are shown shooting the cannons at Fort Edward, and then posing with the city in the background. Gaudet (1889–1906) was a member of the 1st Prince Edward Island contingent to the South African War. He also served as a Sergeant Major in World War I.

BISLEY SHOOTER A CHAMPION, c.1908

Major J. M. "Bisley" Jones of Charlottetown qualified for the Bisley team on eight occasions and represented Canada five times between 1905 and 1912. He became fondly known as "Bisley" because of his accomplishments. Major Jones is shown to the immediate left of the scoreboard (seated, centre).

In 1951, Lieutenant Mary MacLennan of Charlottetown became the first woman to compete at Bisley.

CECILY JANE GEORGINA FANE POPE, C.1890

Matron Nursing Sister Cecily Jane Georgina Fane Pope with the Royal Red Cross. Born in Charlottetown January 1, 1862, and daughter of the Honourable William H. Pope, she designed the first Canadian nurses uniform while serving in the Boer War. She also served in World War I from 1914 to 1919, and she was the first matron to be appointed to the permanent corps of Canadian Nursing Sisters.

This was a scene repeated many, many times as Charlottetown sent young graduates of Prince Edward Island's school of nursing off to conflict, not just in the great wars, but every time their services were needed: Hong Kong, North Africa, Korea, Singapore. Nursing graduates joined the Royal Canadian Army Medical Corps or Canadian Military Hospital in Halifax when the two world wars broke out. Working near the front lines, and living in tents, they ministered to war casualties throughout the years of battle. Their work was hectic, often trying, and certainly wrought with distress, as severely injured Canadian soldiers were brought to their field hospitals. The nursing sisters often wished they could do more, although they did accomplish a great deal. Lieutenant (Nursing Sister) Mary Winnifred MacNutt of Charlottetown was the first Canadian nurse in World War II to receive the Royal Red Cross First Class.

TROOPS IN TRAINING, C.1902

One can only wonder if this unstable-looking structure labelled "Engineer's Bridge, Government Pond," was built as part of an exercise by troops of the Charlottetown Engineer Company. From the look of the young boys with their dogs observing the action from shore, this may well have been the case. Many members of the Charlottetown Engineers had been killed at Paardberg in 1900.

Local Garrison off to Defend Cable Stations, c.1914

When World War I broke out in August 1914, volunteers were recruited from the 4th Regiment Canadian Garrison Artillery, Charlottetown, and sent to Canso and Sydney to guard the cable stations there. Because khaki had not yet been provided as the standard colour of the Canadian militia, the soldiers wore blue uniforms with red trim.

The first world war brought changes to how the militia and military operated but did not detract from the number of residents who joined the war effort. The first detachment of volunteers left in August 1914 with an enthusiastic send-off. The first thoroughly Prince Edward Island infantry, the 105th Battalion, as well as the Second Siege Battery and the Eighth Siege Battery soon joined the war effort.

105TH BATTALION (PEI HIGHLANDERS) PAY HEAVY TOLL, C.1916

The Canadian army in Europe became more persistent in calling for recruits in the summer of 1915. A reinforcement company was authorized to be recruited in Prince Edward Island. The response was greater than expected and the company, under Major R. H. Campbell, was extended to battalion strength and called the 105th Battalion (PEI Highlanders) Canadian Expedition Forces. The unit completed recruiting in 1915, did basic training during the winter, and sailed from Charlottetown with 1,028 personnel on June 16, 1916. It was stationed at Valcartier Camp for thirty days and sailed for England on the S.S. *Empress of Britain* on July 15, 1916. The unit went under canvas, trained at Delegate Camp until November and went into Whitley Camp. The 105th Battalion was a well-trained unit and received many favourable reports, serving in many units across France. Six of the unit's officers received the Military Cross and twenty-eight other ranks received the Military Medal. Of the 1,028 who sailed overseas, 218 were killed in action or died of wounds and 415 were wounded in action—a very heavy toll from one unit from the small province of PEI.

CHARLOTTETOWN HERO OF TWO WARS, CAPTAIN FREDERICK THORNTON PETERS, C.1918

Born in 1889, the son of Honourable Frederick Peters, a former premier of PEI, he joined the Royal Navy in 1905 at age sixteen, and at the outbreak of World War I, held the rank of lieutenant. Retiring in 1919 at the age of thirty, he rejoined in 1939, this time in command of an anti-submarine flotilla. In 1940, he attained the rank of captain. In the attack of Oran in 1942, Captain Peters led two naval cutters through point-blank fire from the Vichy French shore batteries in a suicidal charge against the boom guarding the harbour. His own ship, the *Walney* rammed the boom, sank the destroyer, and attacked the cruiser, but was disabled by its guns from stem to stern and went down in the harbour with the white ensign flying. Captain Peters was the sole survivor, having lost one eye, and was taken prisoner. After the French surrendered after continuing battles, he was freed. A month later, he was killed in an airplane crash while on a special mission. In May 1943, he was awarded the Victoria Cross and the United States Distinguished Service Cross posthumously.

LIGHT HORSE CAVALRY, C.1930

In 1901, the Prince Edward Island Light Horse was formed as a cavalry regiment. Training took place at Falconwood. In the early years this small regiment was used mainly for ceremonial purposes. There are very few photographs that show actual horses. This image was taken at Aldershot Camp, where Lieutenant Colonel G. E. Full was commanding officer.

RENAISSANCE MAN, "COLONEL DAN," c.1925

Lieutenant Colonel D. A. MacKinnon was a druggist, fox breeder, distance runner, rifleman, newspaper owner, racetrack owner, harness racing driver, member of the Canadian Sports Hall of Fame, and courageous soldier. During the first world war, he won the Distinguished Service Order, the French Croix de Guerre with palm, and the Belgian Croix de Guerre. He joined the militia in 1901 and served as a gunner with the 4th Regiment, Canadian Artillery, became captain with the No. 4 Battery in 1904, and later captain of the No. 2 Heavy Battery. He served as a major with the 36th Battery and was in France and Flanders to the end of the WWI. At the end of hostilities he came to PEI to have just as successful a life, and became famous around the Maritimes as "Colonel Dan," of the beloved harness racing track.

ROYAL THANKS TO VETERANS, C.1939

Their Majesties, King George V and Queen Elizabeth, chat with disabled veterans of World War I during a visit to Charlottetown in 1939.

The Soldiers' Monument, a First World War memorial was placed in Queen Square in 1925. During dedication services it was unveiled by Mrs. John MacLean, whose daughter Nursing Sister Rena MacLean made the supreme sacrifice.

BRIGADIER GENERAL PEAKE, c.1945

Charlottetown native Brigadier General G. C. K. Peake became famous by converting an anti-aircraft weapon into an infantry weapon for use with special sniping tasks. He started his career as a private in the Signal Corps and later became a captain in the Artillery Brigade at the outbreak of World War II. Soon after, he took on the task of recruiting the 8th Medium Battery RCA. He went overseas in 1941 with the 2nd Canadian Infantry Division to Europe where he won the Distinguished Service Order. At one stage of his military career, when the Canadians required additional infantry brigades, he was suddenly shoved into the role of commanding officer of an infantry, which required a reorganization of his own unit with additional troops. While overseas he developed and produced special sights for the Befors which enabled them to be used in a ground role.

CHARLOTTETOWN AIR BASE FROM ABOVE, c.1940

An overhead view of the Charlottetown air base operated by the RAF (Royal Air Force of England) and RCAF (Royal Canadian Air Force). World War II impacted strongly on Charlottetown because of the presence of the "boys in blue." Uplands Airport was transformed for the purpose of training airmen ready to battle in the skies over Europe. The No. 2 Air Navigation School at Charlottetown was open for just over four years. When it closed in 1945, it had graduated 1,120 air navigation and 80 air bombers for the RAF and RCAF. The presence of daring young men from England, Canada, the United States, and other countries certainly impacted on the social scene. We hear a lot about war brides coming to Canada, but there was also a flow of war grooms into Prince Edward Island.

Guests Of Prince Edward Island Greeted By Lieutenant Governor

Prior to their being placed in strict quarantine by the Department of Public Health as a precautionary measure, the twenty-five children who arrived in this Province from England were called upon by His Honor Lt. Governor LePage who treated them to ice cream and took them for short rides in his car. The children were greatly pleased and voted the Governor a jolly good sport. Another week must elapse before they leave their present quarters at Mrs. Edwin Stewart's, Bellevue, for the homes of their wartime foster parents throughout the Province. From left to right the names are: Lt. Governor LePage, Miss Phyllis Reay, nurse, Miss Helen Lawson, assistant. Second row standing: Henry Austin, 12, Michael Dale, 10, Cyril Hinshelwood, 12, Gordon Taylor, 14, Tony Kissinger, 14, David Cornish, 12, Miss Jessie Fullerton, Camp Chief, George Newton, 13, Peter Raven, 12, Albert Newton, 12. Third row: Olive Pitt, 9, Neil Foster, 9, Peter Lynn, 8, Doris French, 12, Patricia French, 10, Audrey Pitt, 15, Doris Hare, 11, Brenda Griffin, 13, Margaret Martin, 12. Front row: Malcolm Joyce, 7, Stella Pickering, 6, Barbara Pickering, 8, Shirley Lynn, 5, Mary Roberts, 8, Pamela Foster, 5, Francis Roberts, 6.

EVACUEES FROM ENGLAND, C.1943

These children, evacuated from England to ensure their safety during World War II, were greeted by Lieutenant-Governor LePage. He treated them to ice cream and took them for short rides in his car prior to their being placed in strict quarantine by the department of public health. After their quarantine the children were placed in wartime foster homes until it was safe to return to England. Sending children to Canada was not new to World War II, for between 1869 and the late 1930s, over one hundred thousand juvenile migrants were sent to Canada from Great Britain during the child emigration movement. Motivated by social and economic forces, churches and philanthropic organizations sent orphaned, abandoned, and poor children to Canada. Many believed that these children would have a better chance for a healthy, moral life in rural Canada, where families welcomed them as a source of cheap farm labour and domestic help.

TRAINING NOT TO BE TAKEN LIGHTLY, C.1944

Being a military pilot was a dangerous business both when training and in the combat that followed. There were several crashes recorded at the Charlottetown base that resulted in loss of life. Fortunately one of the more spectacular incidents proved the skill of the aircrew. Those who inspected the damage incurred when this Mark I Anson aircraft "picked up a tree" outside of Souris were amazed that it made it back to Charlottetown. A board of inquiry determined the aircraft was totally un-airworthy from the moment it struck the trees and that it must have required miraculous handling on the part of the pilot to prevent disaster on the fifty-mile return trip to Charlottetown. Others were not so lucky. In 1944 an Anson from the No. 2 Air Navigation School at Charlottetown crashed near the junction of St. Peter's and Norwood roads, killing several airmen from England and New Brunswick. The victims are buried at the Sherwood Cemetery adjacent to the present airport. Three men survived the crash. As dangerous as training was, and as challenging the battles that awaited, the boys in blue held their time in Charlottetown as precious memories. These images were donated by Errol Laughlin, the only native Islander who flew out of Charlottetown with the No. 2 Air Navigation School. He was a staff wireless operator.

ENJOYING THEIR R&R, c.1945

A popular hangout often referred to by resident Islanders and those training at the Charlottetown Air Base was Milton's Old Spain, a local tea room. It compensated in a small way for the fact that there were no pubs due to prohibition.

In January of 1944 the final issue of *G.R.A.F.*, a magazine published by the Royal Air Force for servicemen stationed in Charlottetown, bid farewell to the Island:

> Most of us will find after a few months that we shall be looking back with pleasure to our stay on "The Island." We may even miss the familiar "Friendly Voice of the Maritimes" and a certain old-time band, not for furious fiddling; and we may dwell on the memories of Ed's bus and of enormous suppers at the "Old Spain." We shall remember the red cliffs and the beaches, the colours of maple trees in the autumn and the jingle of sleigh bells in the winter. Then there are the friends we have made amongst the good burghers of Charlottetown, people who have opened their hearts and their homes to us. We shall not forget them.

G.R.A.F.'s Final Farewell, c.1944

The publication of this last issue of the "Graff" coincided with the closing down of the station as an RAF organization.

The Airman's Xmas, 1943

The air base was handed over to the RCAF and within a short few years, Islanders were welcoming their own citizens—and many new ones in the form of war brides—home. A new era started for Charlottetown following World War II, but the city was always made stronger by the memories of the achievements of generations that had gone before.

Selected Bibliography

Atkinson, Ron H., W. A. Beer, and Harry K. Simmonds. *A Treasure Called Belvedere. A Century of Activity at the Charlottetown Golf Club*. Charlottetown: Belvedere Golf Club, 2002.

Bruce, Harry. *Maud: The Early Years of L.M. Montgomery*. Halifax: Nimbus Publishing Ltd., 2003.

Confederation Birthplace Commission. *Powerful Memories Powerful Dreams: Final Report of the Confederation Birthplace Commission*. Charlottetown, 1991.

Douglas, R. *Place-Names of Prince Edward Island*. Ottawa: Dominion of Canada, 1925.

Graham, Allan. *A Photo History of the Prince Edward Island Railway*. Summerside: Allan Graham, 2001.

Hornby, Jim. *Black Islanders*. Charlottetown: Institute of Island Studies, University of Prince Edward Island, 1991.

Historic Society of Prince Edward Island. *Historic Sidelights*. Charlottetown: Historic Society of Prince Edward Island, 1956.

MacIntyre, Wendell. "The Irish." Vol. 3. *The Abegweit Review*. Charlottetown: University of Prince Edward Island, 1988.

Scott Smith, H.M. *The Historic Churches of Prince Edward Island*. Charlottetown: SSP Publications, 1986.

Weale, David. *A Stream Out of Lebanon: An Introduction to the Coming of Syrian/Lebanese Emigrants to Prince Edward Island*. Charlottetown: Institute of Island Studies, 1988.

Image Sources

Numbers refer to page numbers in the text.

Charlottetown Fire Department: 89;

City of Charlottetown: 6, 95 (top);

Confederation Centre Art Gallery: 110;

Julie V. Watson: 107;

Library and Archives Canada: 8, 17, 19, 22, 23, 24, 25, 33, 34, 39, 41, 48, 49, 57, 64, 74, 85, 105, 106, 111, 124 (top), 125, 138.

Image on page 19 copyright Library and Archives Canada. Reproduced with permission of the Minister of Public Works and Government Services Canada (2006).

All other images courtesy Public Archives and Records Office of Prince Edward Island, accession numbers are listed below:

Page 1 Acc2320/9-3, Acc2320/9-6;
Page 2 Acc2320/9-18;
Page 3 Acc2320/57-5;
Page 4 Acc2320/6-4, Acc2320/6-5;
Page 5 Acc2320/6-8;
Page 7 Map 0,534;
Page 9 Acc2320/54-7;
Page 10 Acc2320/54-12;
Page 11 Acc2320/54-4, Acc2320/54-8;
Page 12 Acc2320/55-6;
Page 13 Acc2320/55-7;
Page 14 Acc2320/35-8;
Page 15 Acc4249/1;
Page 20 Acc2755/102;
Page 21 Acc3862/4;

Page 27 Acc3466/HF78.72.23;
Page 28 Acc2301/274;
Page 29 Acc2320/56-7;
Page 30 Acc2702/s23/3;
Page 31 Acc4170/75;
Page 32 Acc2702/s23/10;
Page 35 Acc3879/14;
Page 37 Acc2301/224a;
Page 38 Acc3885/6;
Page 40 Acc2320/57-6;
Page 42 Acc2301/22;
Page 43 Acc2874/8;
Page 44 Acc4567/2;
Page 45 Acc3466/HF77.34;
Page 46 Acc2320/30-8;

Page 47 Acc2301/91;
Page 50 Acc4390/75a;
Page 51 Acc2320/25-2;
Page 52 Acc2320/25-9;
Page 53 Acc2320/25-17;
Page 54 Acc2320/25-10;
Page 55 Acc2320/26-1;
Page 56 Acc4466/2;
Page 58 Acc4261/9;
Page 59 Acc2320/64-14, Acc2320/64-17;
Page 60 Acc2320/64-15;
Page 61 Acc2320/28-3;
Page 62 Acc2320/63-2;
Page 63 Acc3466/HF70.1778.3.2;
Page 65 Acc2305/10;
Page 66 Acc2320/66-16;
Page 67 Acc3466/HF73.354.2;
Page 68 Acc2320/88-10;
Page 69 Acc2320/27-6;
Page 70 Acc2320/27-8;
Page 71 Acc2320/27-7;
Page 72 Acc2320/28-4;
Page 73 Acc3523/56, Acc3523/57;
Page 75 Acc3523/100;
Page 76 Acc3523/151;
Page 77 Acc3523/175;
Page 78 Acc3523/43;
Page 79 Acc2320/64-6;
Page 80 Acc4339/1;
Page 81 Acc4562/1;
Page 82 Acc2320/18-6;
Page 83 Acc3466/HF76.50.3;
Page 84 Acc4552/3;
Page 86 Acc2320/19A-11;
Page 87 Acc2320/21-1;
Page 88 Acc2320/88-1;
Page 90 Acc2301/278;
Page 91 Acc4552/8, Acc4552/13;
Page 92 Acc2320/90-10;
Page 93 Acc2320/65-1;
Page 94 Acc2320/90-3;
Page 95 Acc3466/HF76.57.5;

Page 96 Acc2320/17-3;
Page 97 Acc3845/1;
Page 98 Acc2320/42-8;
Page 99 Acc3218/80;
Page 100 Acc2846/3;
Page 101 Acc2301/17;
Page 102 Acc2320/51-8;
Page 103 Acc2320/51-2;
Page 104 Acc2986/1;
Page 108 Acc2301/244;
Page 109 Acc2320/38-1;
Page 112 Acc2320/58-3
Page 113 Acc3466/HF74.27.3.12, Acc3466/HF74.27.3.189;
Page 114 Acc2320/50-8;
Page 115 Acc2996/1, Acc2320/49-5;
Page 116 Acc2320/22-5;
Page 117 Acc2320/70-7;
Page 118 Acc2320/46-7;
Page 119 Acc2301/94;
Page 120 Acc2320/83-1;
Page 121 Acc2986/2;
Page 122 Acc2320/85-5;
Page 123 Acc2320/86-4;
Page 124 Acc2320/96-4;
Page 126 Acc2702/s23/90;
Page 127 Acc3466/HF82.22.7;
Page 128 Acc2320/92-2;
Page 129 Acc2301/10, Acc2320/92-5;
Page 130 Acc2320/98-5;
Page 131 Acc2320/70-3;
Page 132 Acc2320/73-5;
Page 133 Acc4359/2;
Page 134 Acc3466/HF78.72.28;
Page 135 Acc2320/73-7;
Page 136 Acc2320/55-8;
Page 137 Acc2320/55-11;
Page 139 Acc2301/279;
Page 140 Acc2320/98-6;
Page 141 Acc2330/H-87;
Page 142 Acc2301/76;
Page 143 Acc2320/32-8, Acc2320/32-11;

Page 144 Acc2320/32-14;
Page 145 Acc2320/32-12;
Page 146 Acc2320/39-1;
Page 147 Acc2320/41-11;
Page 148 Acc2320/41-12;
Page 149 Acc2702/Series23/89;
Page 150 Acc4516/3;
Page 151 Acc2320/102-11;
Page 152 Acc4516/1, Acc4516/2;
Page 153 Acc2320/79-10;
Page 154 Acc2320/103-3;
Page 155 Acc2320/103-10;
Page 156 Acc2320/104-6, Acc2320/105-1;
Page 158 Acc2320/110-4, Acc2320/118-2;
Page 159 Acc2320/106-1;
Page 160 Acc2320/110-7;
Page 161 Acc2320/118-16;
Page 162 Acc3955/4;
Page 163 Acc4770/s4/19;
Page 164 Acc3955/3;
Page 165 Acc2843/2;
Page 166 Acc2415/2a, Acc2415/2a;